blue prints

Maths *Key Stage 2*
Pupil Resource Book

Sean McArdle

Text © Sean McArdle 2002
Original illustrations © Nelson Thornes Ltd 2002

Published in 2002 by:
Nelson Thornes Ltd
Delta Place
27 Bath Road
CHELTENHAM
GL53 7TH
United Kingdom

01 02 03 04 05 / 10 9 8 7 6 5 4 3 2 1

A catalogue record for this book is available from the British Library

ISBN 0 7487 6373 2

Printed and bound in Great Britain by The Bath Press

Contents

Contents

Introduction

These activity sheets are designed to help with the delivery of the National Numeracy Strategy. They work alongside the *Blueprints Maths Key Stage 2: Teacher's Resource Book* in this series for Key Stage 2 and cover material which directly relates to the latest mathematics curriculum.

Many of the activity sheets may be used by a whole class but others are more suitable for particular ability groups. Clearly, their use will vary from school to school, from teacher to teacher and from class to class. Where modifications are needed, the activity sheets can often be easily changed or offer a basis for differentiation.

The activity sheets are supplemented by a variety of the most commonly required activity sheet blanks such as squared paper in various sizes and number squares. Record sheets for class teachers and supply teachers are also included.

Activity sheets

Each activity sheet in *Blueprints Maths Key Stage 2: Pupil Resource Book* is linked to an activity page in *Blueprints Maths Key Stage 2: Teacher's Resource Book*. The link is made explicit through the numbers in the hand prints in each book. Each activity sheet is designed to assist the theme and is offered as a possible activity in order to save preparation time.

It should also be noted that not all the activity sheets include explicit instructions for the children to follow. Such instructions that do appear can only be abbreviated guidelines. Irrespective of any printed instruction, the children will, of course, follow your own instructions and explanations of the activity they are to undertake.

Activity sheet number in the hand print in the *Pupil Resource Book* also on the relevant page (top left) in the *Teacher's Resource Book*

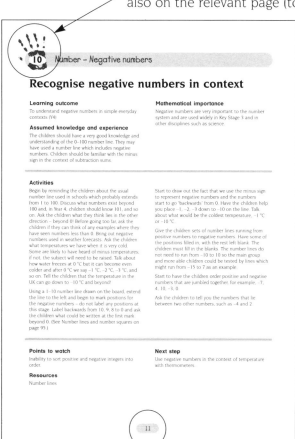

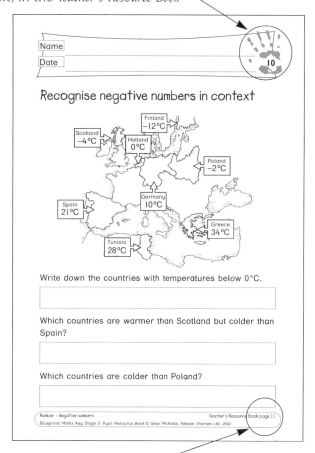

Linked *Teacher's Resource Book* page number appears in the bottom-right corner of the relevant activity sheet in the *Pupil Resource Book*

Counting on or back in tens or hundreds

Put each group in order (smallest first) and then write the next three numbers.

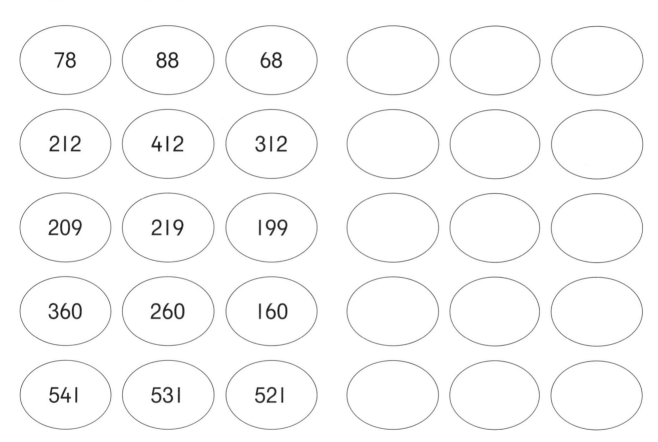

78 88 68

212 412 312

209 219 199

360 260 160

541 531 521

Put each group in order (largest first) and then write the next three numbers.

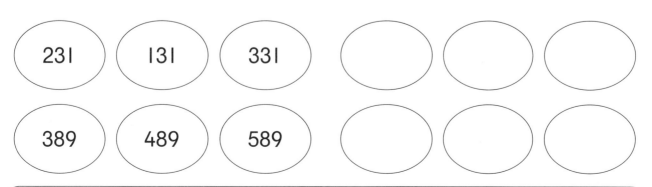

231 131 331

389 489 589

Counting in equal steps and in decimals

Continue each sequence.

25	50	75	100	___	___	___	___	___
175	200	225	250	___	___	___	___	___
775	750	725	700	___	___	___	___	___
150	125	100	75	___	___	___	___	___
3	28	53	78	___	___	___	___	___
19	44	69	94	___	___	___	___	___
112	87	62	37	___	___	___	___	___
456	481	506	531	___	___	___	___	___
3.4	3.5	3.6	3.7	___	___	___	___	___
12.2	12.3	12.4	12.5	___	___	___	___	___
0.7	0.6	0.5	0.4	___	___	___	___	___
100.0	99.9	99.8	99.7	___	___	___	___	___
42	60	78	96	___	___	___	___	___
71	55	39	23	___	___	___	___	___
945	972	999	___	___	___	___	___	

Read/write whole numbers to 1000/10 000

Which year? Write in the numbers.

Two hundred and thirteen

Ten hundred and sixty-six

Fifteen hundred and nine

Lots of money. Write in the words.

Know what each digit represents

Circle the 'tens' value.

264   80   512   706

75   32   196   437

Circle the 'units' value.

36   8   121   206

90   493   357   42

Complete each sequence. (The first is done for you.)

400 >	20 >	8 >	428 >
200 >	30 >	4 >	
>	80 >	6 >	786 >
>	30 >	>	635 >

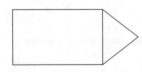
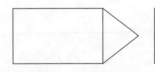

Show each number on an abacus by drawing beads on the columns.

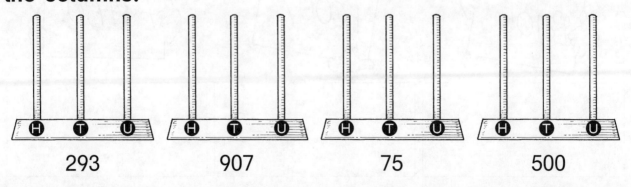

293   907   75   500

Order whole numbers to 1000

Circle the bigger number in each pair.

345   261   418   636   869   576   590   375

230   203   412   421   967   697   426   264

Circle the most money in each group of three.

31p   65p   46p   76p   42p   80p   £129   £360   £850

£730   £703   £370   130p   65p   89p   110p   60p   95p

Write down the even numbers between each pair.

121 _____ 130

65 _____ 80

Circle the smaller amount in each pair.

2.5 kg   4.1 kg   52 cm   58 cm   130 cm   103 cm

Write each group of numbers again with the smallest first.

524   254   542   245   452   _____

607   760   706   670   76   _____

Use symbols correctly including < and >

Draw the correct sign (< or >) in each number sequence to make it true.

7	14	11	9	15p	34p
8 cm	5 cm	20 cm	5 cm	50p	70p
£1.30	105p	56	65	32g	23g
205p	£2.50	416	461	409	490
281 cm	218 cm	$\frac{1}{2}$	$\frac{3}{4}$		

Write a number so that each sentence is true.

14   <   _____   250   >   _____

_____   >   5 cm   £3.00   <   _____

$5\frac{1}{2}$ >   _____   _____   <   2p

Order all symbols and to one million

Lottery winners! How much might each person receive?

Sort it! Use either >, = or < to show the relationship between each pair.

£315 000   £350 000   £705 000   £695 000

£15 000   £13 900   2975p   £29.75

20 000 g   17 kg   250 m   25 000 cm

Complete each relationship with a suitable amount.

450 000 < _____   £300 > _____ p

40m < _____ cm   3 hours = _____ mins

Write the numbers in order, smallest first.

25 456   206 000   120 000   _____   _____   _____

7 450   64 500   50 450   _____   _____   _____

| Name | .... |
| Date | .... |

8

Order positive and negative integers

Look at the clown's numbers.

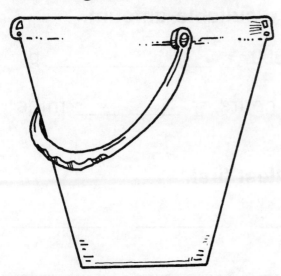

−6

12

−4

0

3

−8

7

5

−1

−10

10

−5

Write the correct numbers for each bucket.

The negative numbers

The positive numbers

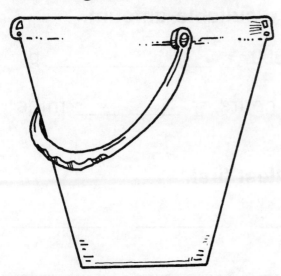

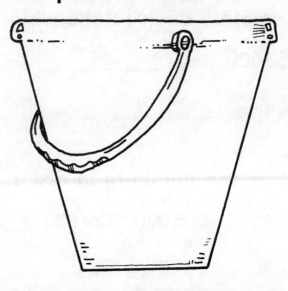

Rounding to nearest ten and hundred

Round to the nearest ten

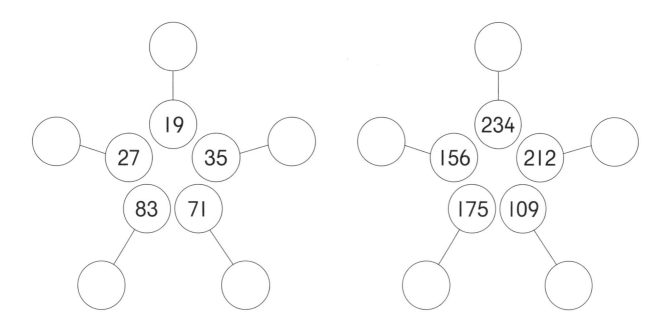

Round to the nearest hundred

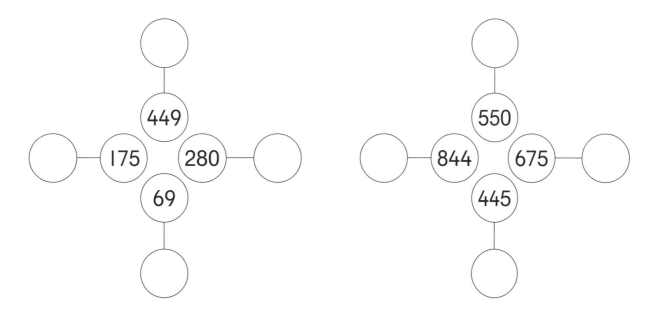

Recognise negative numbers in context

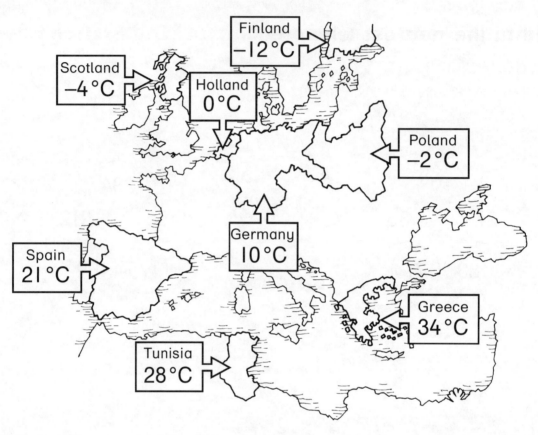

Write down the countries with temperatures below 0°C.

Which countries are warmer than Scotland but colder than Spain?

Which countries are colder than Poland?

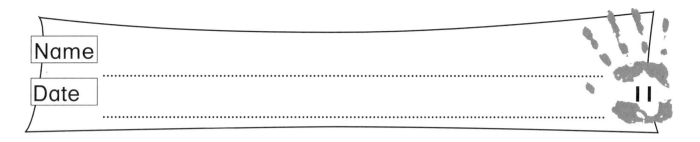

Positive and negative integers

Find the difference between each pair. The first one has been done for you.

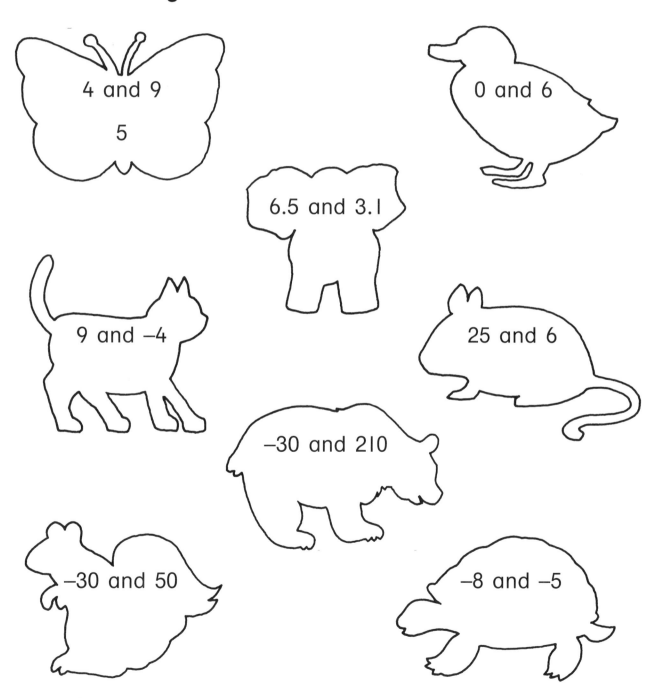

4 and 9

5

0 and 6

6.5 and 3.1

9 and −4

25 and 6

−30 and 210

−30 and 50

−8 and −5

Number – Negative numbers

Teacher's Resource Book page 12

Blueprints Maths Key Stage 2: Pupil Resource Book © Sean McArdle, Nelson Thornes Ltd, 2002

Unit fractions

Each child gives a quarter of their money to charity. How much do they give?

Sanchez	Maria	Alfonse	Danielle

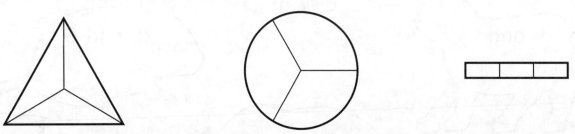

One third of each pattern needs to be coloured red.

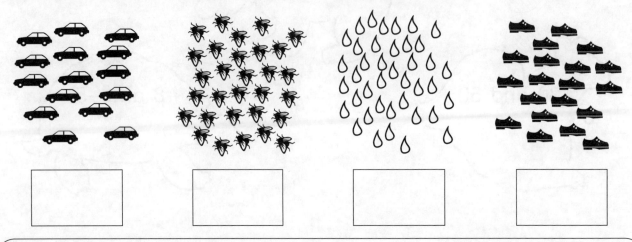

Write in each box one-fifth of each amount.

Simple fractions/equivalence

What fraction of each group is shaded?

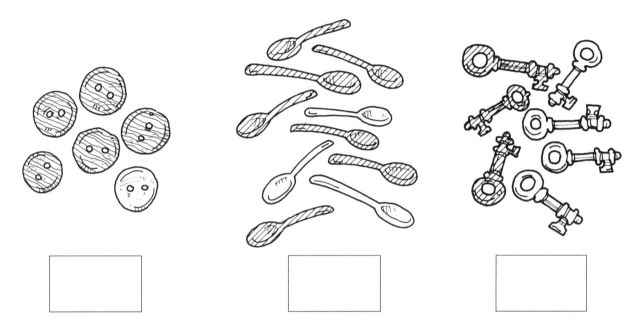

Write in two ways what fraction of each group is shaded.

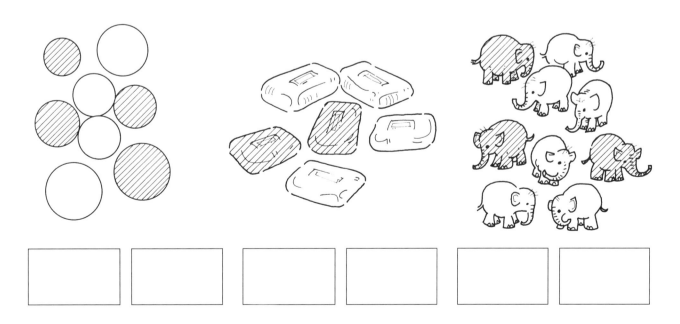

Simple fractions/find fractional parts

Write each row of fractions in order, smallest first.

$\frac{3}{4}$ $\frac{1}{2}$ $\frac{1}{10}$ $\frac{1}{4}$ =   ___   ___   ___   ___

$\frac{3}{5}$ $\frac{1}{5}$ $\frac{4}{5}$ $\frac{2}{5}$ =   ___   ___   ___   ___

$\frac{1}{4}$ $\frac{1}{3}$ $\frac{1}{2}$ $\frac{1}{10}$ =   ___   ___   ___   ___

$\frac{4}{10}$ $\frac{2}{10}$ $\frac{9}{10}$ $\frac{5}{10}$ =   ___   ___   ___   ___

Write $\frac{1}{4}$ of 12 ___   20 ___   40 ___   16 ___   32 ___

Write $\frac{1}{3}$ of 15 ___   9 ___   21 ___   18 ___   30 ___

Write $\frac{1}{5}$ of 20 ___   5 ___   30 ___   45 ___   25 ___

Write $\frac{1}{10}$ of 60 ___   10 ___   100 ___   30 ___   80 ___

Write $\frac{1}{3}$ of 12 kg ___   24 kg ___   3 kg ___   300 kg ___

Two-thirds of a number is 8. What is the number? ____

Nine-tenths of a number is 18. What is the number? ____

Four-fifths of a number is 16. What is the number? ____

A quarter of a number is 5. What is three-quarters? ____

A fifth of a number is 7. What is three-fifths? ____

A tenth of a number is 5. What is nine-tenths? ____

Blueprints Maths Key Stage 2: Pupil Resource Book © Sean McArdle, Nelson Thornes Ltd, 2002

Begin to use ideas of simple proportion

Children spend 5 days at school each week. How many days do these children spend at school?

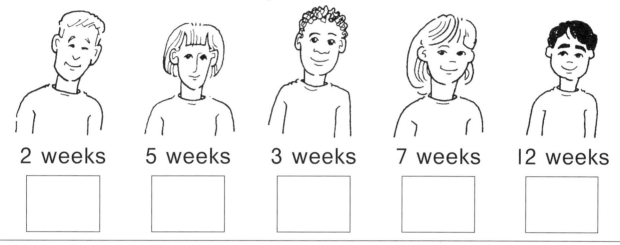

| 2 weeks | 5 weeks | 3 weeks | 7 weeks | 12 weeks |

How many certificates? The children receive a certificate for every 5 house points.

| 20 points | 35 points | 100 points | 15 points | 80 points |

The children receive 2 sweets for every 3 correct answers. How many sweets?

9 correct answers

30 correct answers

Mixed numbers and improper fractions

Change the improper fractions to mixed numbers.

$\frac{3}{2}$ =

$\frac{5}{2}$ =

$\frac{9}{2}$ =

$\frac{7}{3}$ =

$\frac{12}{3}$ =

$\frac{30}{3}$ =

$\frac{40}{4}$ =

$\frac{17}{4}$ =

$\frac{36}{4}$ =

Change the mixed numbers to improper fractions.

$3\frac{1}{2}$ =

$7\frac{1}{2}$ =

$9\frac{1}{2}$ =

$26\frac{1}{2}$ =

$4\frac{1}{3}$ =

$9\frac{1}{3}$ =

$12\frac{2}{3}$ =

$20\frac{2}{3}$ =

$12\frac{3}{5}$ =

Write each of these in at least 2 different ways. The first one has been done for you.

$4\frac{1}{2}$ $\frac{9}{2}$ 4.5

3.7

Reduce fractions by cancelling

Some of these fractions are far too complicated. Make each fraction as simple as you can.

$\frac{4}{16}$ =

$\frac{5}{50}$ =

$\frac{7}{14}$ =

$\frac{9}{10}$ =

$\frac{12}{18}$ =

$\frac{2}{100}$ =

$\frac{4}{24}$ =

$\frac{12}{15}$ =

$\frac{90}{100}$ =

$\frac{11}{66}$ =

$\frac{9}{36}$ =

$\frac{21}{24}$ =

$\frac{7}{35}$ =

$\frac{4}{30}$ =

$\frac{6}{15}$ =

$\frac{3}{25}$ =

$\frac{18}{54}$ =

$\frac{14}{84}$ =

$\frac{5}{18}$ =

$\frac{24}{30}$ =

$\frac{19}{36}$ =

Blueprints Maths Key Stage 2: Pupil Resource Book © Sean McArdle, Nelson Thornes Ltd, 2002

Relate fractions to division

Find $\frac{1}{4}$ of each amount.

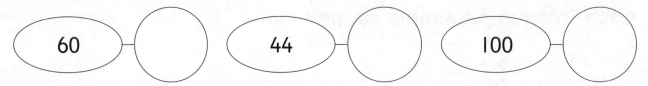

Divide each amount by 4.

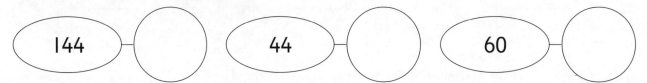

Find $\frac{1}{5}$ of each amount.

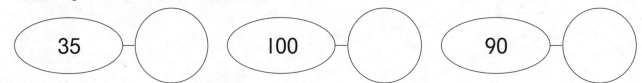

Divide each amount by 5.

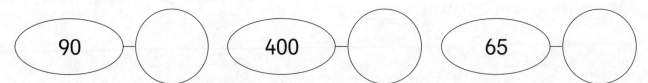

Find $\frac{1}{3}$ of each amount.

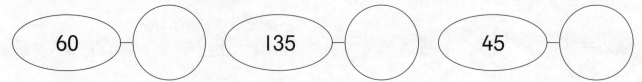

Divide each amount by 3.

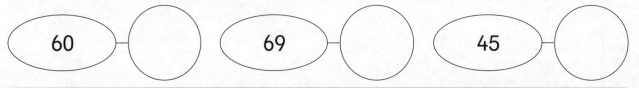

Decimal notation for tenths and hundredths

Write the decimal form of each of these fractions.

$\frac{3}{10}$ _____ $\frac{7}{100}$ _____ $\frac{2}{10}$ _____ $\frac{5}{100}$ _____

$\frac{1}{10}$ _____ $\frac{90}{100}$ _____ $\frac{4}{10}$ _____ $\frac{20}{100}$ _____

$\frac{5}{10}$ _____ $\frac{70}{100}$ _____ $\frac{9}{10}$ _____ $\frac{6}{10}$ _____

Place these decimals on the number line.

1.3   0.7   2.1   1.8   0.2   2.5   1.5   0.4   2.9

0					1					2					3

Convert these pounds into pennies.

£1.65 _____   £2.73 _____   £5.50 _____   £1.09 _____

Convert these pennies into pounds.

205p _____   341p _____   560p _____   56p _____

Put these in order, smallest first.

3.12   2.84   0.65   5.07   _____ _____ _____ _____

Order numbers with three decimal places

Write a decimal between each pair.

1.25 _____ 1.26   3.01 _____ 3.02   2.76 _____ 2.77

Convert each amount into the units shown.

2.751 km in metres   3.75 litres in millilitres

_____   _____

5.0 kg in grams   0.06 litres in millilitres

_____   _____

Arrange these according to size, smallest first.

2.67 m   0.856 m   0.76 m   12.531 m   _____

2.485 kg   24.851 kg   0.248 kg   2.048 kg   _____

5.051 m   0.551 m   50.51 m   5.51 m   _____

20.454   20.7   20.054   20.07   _____

1.5   5.1   1.049   5.049   _____

0.321   0.041   0.009   0.101   _____

Equivalence between decimals and fractions

Join up the amounts that mean the same.

$\frac{1}{4}$

nought point one

one-fifth

0.25

nought point seven five

nought point two

0.333

one-quarter

one-tenth

$\frac{1}{5}$

0.2

0.1

0.75

three-quarters

one-third

nought point two five

$\frac{1}{3}$

$\frac{1}{10}$

nought point three three three

$\frac{3}{4}$

Round two decimal places to nearest integer

Round each amount to the nearest pound.

£1.67 ⬜   £2.94 ⬜   £1.34 ⬜

£2.46 ⬜   £3.52 ⬜   £4.48 ⬜

Round each amount to the nearest metre.

2.45 m ⬜   3.12 m ⬜   18.60 m ⬜

45.05 m ⬜   6.50 m ⬜   30.4 m ⬜

Round each amount to the nearest kilogram.

2.8 kg ⬜   7.2 kg ⬜   0.90 kg ⬜

6.5 kg ⬜   0.5 kg ⬜   12.5 kg ⬜

Round each amount to the nearest whole litre.

5.55 l ⬜   2.96 l ⬜   3.61 l ⬜

12.2 l ⬜   15.45 l ⬜   0.83 l ⬜

Percentage as number of parts in 100

Write 50% of each amount.

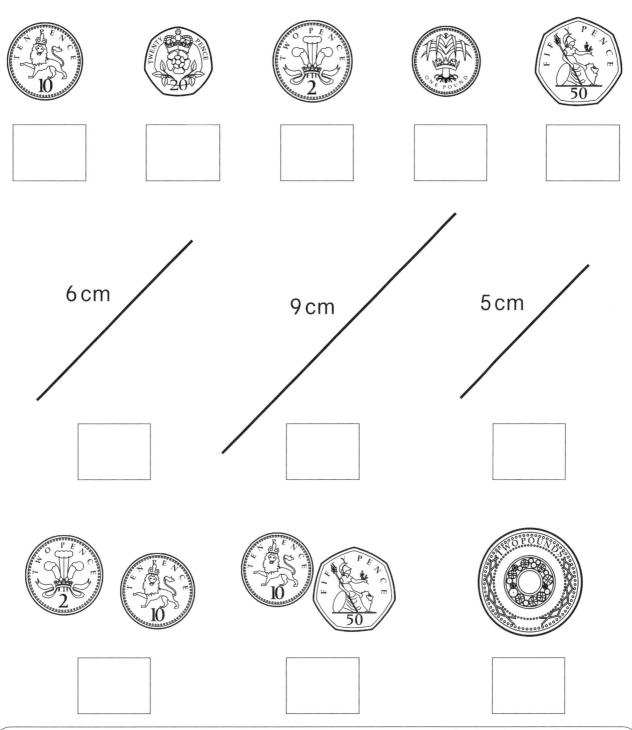

Blueprints Maths Key Stage 2: Pupil Resource Book © Sean McArdle, Nelson Thornes Ltd, 2002

Percentages of small whole numbers

Write each percentage both as a decimal and a fraction.

25%

40%

68%

10%

75%

18%

Circle the amounts that are less than one-quarter.

75% $\frac{2}{3}$ 0.4   10% $\frac{1}{5}$ 0.2 $\frac{7}{10}$

Work out each amount. Use a calculator if you need to.

Find 15% of £360

Find 60% of £400

Positive and negative facts to 20

Write the addition pairs for each number.

16

17

Complete each number sentence.

$14 - 8 =$ ☆ $17 - 9 =$ ☆ $7 + 8 =$ ☆

$9 + 6 =$ ☆ $15 - 6 =$ ☆ $17 - 12 =$ ☆

$20 - 6 =$ ☆ $19 - 14 =$ ☆ $16 - 4 =$ ☆

$15 - 12 =$ ☆ $11 + 6 =$ ☆ $10 - 10 =$ ☆

Use informal pencil and paper methods

Jared works out addition like this.

37

+ 18

First I add the tens   30 add 10 is 40

Then I add the units   7 and 8 is 15

Finally I add them together   40 and 15 is 55

Work out these in the same way.

49

+ 25

First add the tens   _____

Now add the units   _____

Add them together   _____

36

+ 57

First add the tens   _____

Now add the units   _____

Add them together   _____

Mandy works out subtraction by adding on like this.

34 – 16

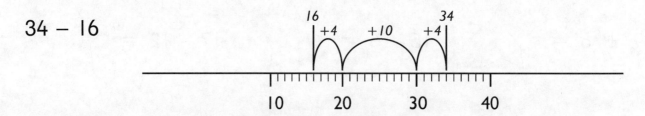

Now work out this subtraction the same way.

75 – 48

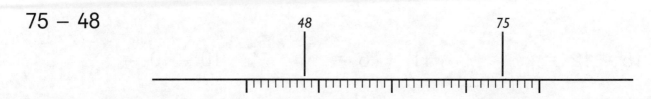

Begin to use column addition

How much does each one have?

Michael

35p
14p

David

12p
17p

Katie

42p
20p

Cindy

18p
21p

Sam

130p
67p

Toni

250p
48p

Jo

155p
36p

Pete

340p
29p

Dolph

255p
125p

Arnie

145p
255p

Maria

505p
340p

Lynne

340p
165p

Blueprints Maths Key Stage 2: Pupil Resource Book © Sean McArdle, Nelson Thornes Ltd, 2002

Name	
Date	

Begin to use column subtraction

How much does each child have left?

Anita

```
   45p
 - 23p
```

Boris

```
   37p
 - 14p
```

Cathy

```
   68p
 - 18p
```

Darius

```
   59p
 -  7p
```

Ingrid

```
   21p
 - 12p
```

Jake

```
   47p
 - 18p
```

Karl

```
   53p
 - 49p
```

Lori

```
   34p
 - 16p
```

Vic

```
   143p
 - 117p
```

Winona

```
   245p
 - 168p
```

Troy

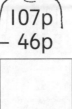
```
   107p
 -  46p
```

Sean

```
   312p
 - 237p
```

Blueprints Maths Key Stage 2: Pupil Resource Book © Sean McArdle, Nelson Thornes Ltd, 2002

Column addition and subtraction

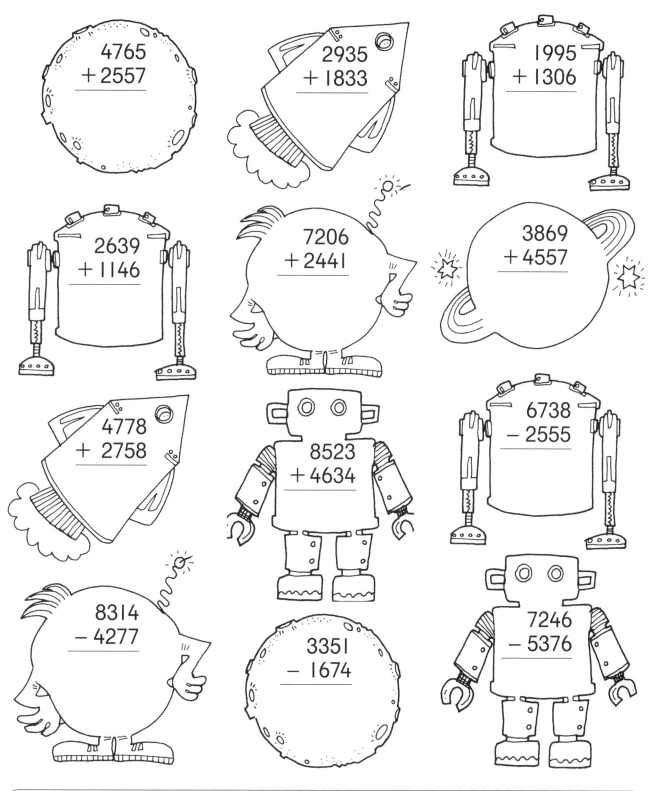

Short and long multiplication, short division

145
× 4

237
× 3

174
× 5

216
× 6

362
× 12

483
× 26

625
× 62

742
× 78

638
× 25

5)245

7)455

6)762

Name

Date

Multiplication with decimals

Deadly decimals! Estimate first, then work them out.

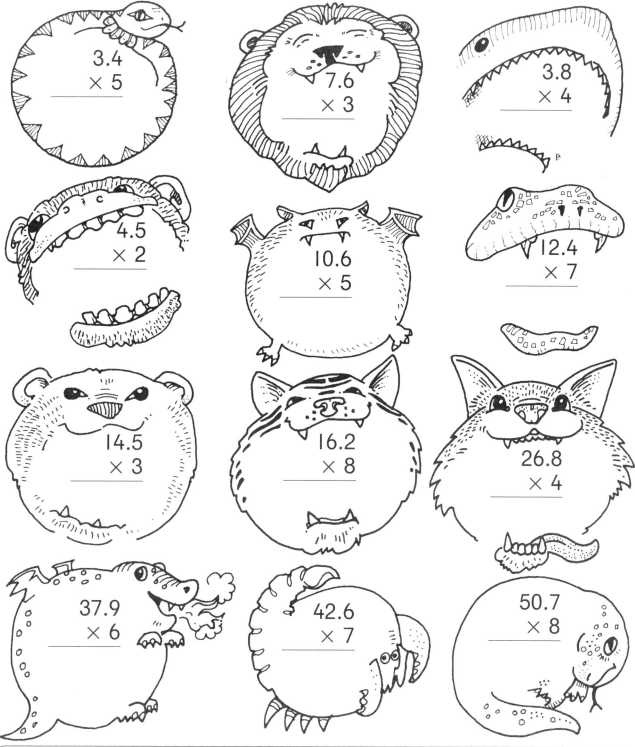

3.4
× 5

7.6
× 3

3.8
× 4

4.5
× 2

10.6
× 5

12.4
× 7

14.5
× 3

16.2
× 8

26.8
× 4

37.9
× 6

42.6
× 7

50.7
× 8

Calculations – Pencil and paper

Blueprints Maths Key Stage 2: Pupil Resource Book © Sean McArdle, Nelson Thornes Ltd, 2002

Short division of numbers involving decimals

Diabolical decimal divisions!

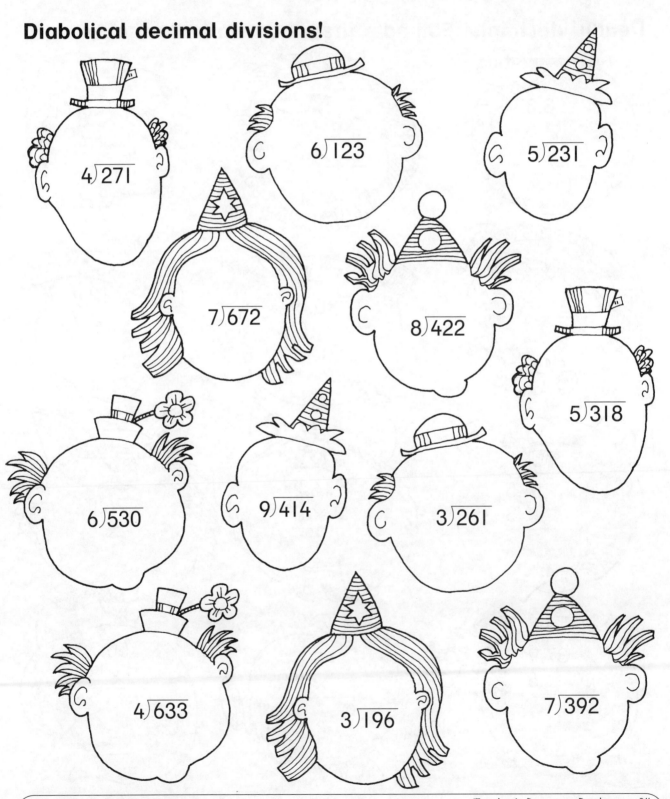

4)271

6)123

5)231

7)672

8)422

5)318

6)530

9)414

3)261

4)633

3)196

7)392

Addition and subtraction of decimals

Dastardly decimals!

£4.32
+ £7.53

£5.12
+ £8.63

£6.27
+ £2.90

£7.38
+ £6.53

£7.94
+ £5.78

£2.06
+ £7.89

£6.45
+ £4.85

£8.38
+ £6.14

£16.45
− £7.65

£32.34
− £18.49

£14.98
− £10.65

£21.15
− £13.83

Approximation methods

It is useful to approximate answers. We could approximate something like 23 × 9 by working out 20 × 10. This would help us check to see if our final answer is correct. **Approximate with each of these multiplications. Only work out the approximate answer!**

19 × 8 =	20	10 =	200
32 × 9 =		=	
17 × 11 =		=	
27 × 9 =		=	
11 × 9 =		=	
36 × 18 =		=	
41 × 19 =		=	
19 × 9 =		=	
21 × 8 =		=	

Blueprints Maths Key Stage 2: Pupil Resource Book © Sean McArdle, Nelson Thornes Ltd, 2002

Calculator skills

Use a calculator to help you answer these questions.
You do not need to show working.

Three consecutive numbers add up to 192.

What are the numbers?

A bottle contains 5 litres of milk. The milk is poured in to 60 ml glasses. How many glasses are filled and how much milk is left?

Glasses filled =   Milk left =

Darius saves 1p on the first of the month, 2p on the second, 4p on the third, 8p on the fourth, and so on.

How much has he saved in total on the 21st of the month?

How much is missing? $7.91 - $ $= 4.77$

Olaf has £1.68. Maria has £2.42. Peggy has an amount halfway between.
How much does Peggy have?

Begin to use brackets

Most of Billy's work is correct but some is not. Put the correct answers alongside the wrong answers.

$3 + (4 \times 2) = 11$

$12 \times (3 \times 2) = 72$

$10 + (4 - 2) = 12$

$8 - (4 \times 2) = 0$

$20 - (10 + 3) = 7$

$20 - (10 + 3) = 17$

$(3 \times 4) + 2 = 18$

$(4 - 2) \times 3 = 6$

$(5 - 4) \times 5 = 5$

$(10 - 6) \times 3 = 12$

$(2 \times 6) - 3 = 6$

$14 - (3 \times 4) = 44$

$16 - (5 + 6) = 11$

$15 + (3 \times 2) = 36$

$9 - (3 + 4) = 2$

$7 - (2 \times 3) = 1$

$2 \times (3 + 5) = 11$

$15 + (10 - 6) = 18$

$12 \times (3 + 2) = 38$

$10 \times (5 - 4) = 46$

$(5 + 3) \times 2 = 16$

$(8 - 3) \times 2 = 2$

$(6 + 3) \times 2 = 18$

$(8 - 5) \times 4 = 12$

$20 + (6 - 2) = 24$

$20 + (5 \times 3) = 75$

$20 - (4 \times 3) = 48$

$60 - (6 + 6) = 60$

Division – inverse of multiplication

Kylie has used these numbers in different ways

$2 \times 3 = 6$

$3 \times 2 = 6$

$6 \div 3 = 2$

$6 \div 2 = 3$

Help Jason do the same thing with these numbers.

$3 \times 4 = 12$

_____

_____

_____

$5 \times 2 = 10$

_____

_____

_____

$4 \times 2 = 8$

_____

_____

_____

$3 \times 5 = 15$

_____

_____

_____

$12 \div 3 = 4$

_____

_____

_____

$20 \div 5 = 4$

_____

_____

_____

$16 \div 2 = 8$

_____

_____

_____

$20 \div 2 = 10$

_____

_____

_____

$5 \times 10 = 50$

_____

_____

_____

Begin to find remainders

Pieces of pizza! The children share the pizza pieces equally. How many bits are left over?

Remainders

If each bird eats five worms, how many worms escape?

The frogs share the dragonflies equally. How many dragonflies escape?

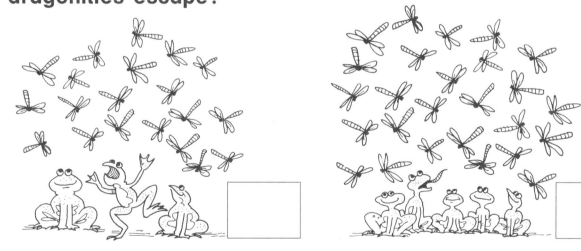

Write down the remainder each time.

50p shared by 3

35p shared by 6

50p shared by 4

2×, 5×, 10× tables/3×, 4× tables

Speed Test (15 seconds)

Test A	Test B	Test C
2 × 5 =	10 × 4 =	4 × 5 =
4 × 10 =	2 × 7 =	3 × 6 =
7 × 2 =	4 × 3 =	2 × 7 =
3 × 4 =	10 × 8 =	10 × 8 =
8 × 10 =	6 × 2 =	5 × 9 =
2 × 6 =	5 × 9 =	4 × 6 =
9 × 5 =	3 × 3 =	3 × 7 =
10 × 10 =	2 × 5 =	2 × 8 =
5 × 2 =	5 × 7 =	10 × 9 =

Total correct   **Total correct**   **Total correct**

Begin to know 6×, 7×, 8× and 9× tables

Speed Test (15 seconds)

Test A	Test B	Test C
$6 \times 4 =$	$3 \times 7 =$	$7 \times 7 =$
$7 \times 3 =$	$5 \times 8 =$	$9 \times 9 =$
$8 \times 5 =$	$2 \times 9 =$	$8 \times 8 =$
$9 \times 2 =$	$7 \times 7 =$	$6 \times 6 =$
$6 \times 6 =$	$9 \times 7 =$	$8 \times 9 =$
$7 \times 9 =$	$7 \times 8 =$	$7 \times 6 =$
$8 \times 7 =$	$5 \times 9 =$	$9 \times 8 =$
$9 \times 5 =$	$9 \times 2 =$	$8 \times 7 =$
$2 \times 9 =$	$8 \times 3 =$	$6 \times 9 =$

Total correct

Total correct

Total correct

Blueprints Maths Key Stage 2: Pupil Resource Book © Sean McArdle, Nelson Thornes Ltd, 2002

All multiplication tables to 10× table

Speed Test (15 seconds)

Test A	Test B	Test C
3 × 4 =	9 × 6 =	2 × 9 =
5 × 9 =	4 × 7 =	3 × 8 =
8 × 7 =	6 × 8 =	4 × 7 =
10 × 3 =	9 × 7 =	5 × 6 =
6 × 9 =	3 × 4 =	6 × 9 =
2 × 8 =	8 × 7 =	7 × 10 =
8 × 4 =	6 × 9 =	8 × 8 =
9 × 6 =	9 × 9 =	9 × 7 =
4 × 7 =	7 × 7 =	5 × 8 =

Total correct   **Total correct**   **Total correct**

Numbers to 20, multiples of 5, 50, halves

Help Sandeep double her money. Write double the amount alongside the money.

32p

16p   2p   400p

30p

14p   25p   16p

200p

1p

5p

150p   2p   4p

15p

90p

30p   14p

6p   18p

17p   34p

35p   80p

All square numbers to 10 × 10/12 × 12

Tick the children who are holding square numbers.

Describe in a sentence what square numbers are.

_____

_____

Blueprints Maths Key Stage 2: Pupil Resource Book © Sean McArdle, Nelson Thornes Ltd, 2002

Factors to 100/prime factors

Write the factors of each gate number.

Describe in a sentence what factors are.

_____

_____

Recognise prime numbers

Circle the prime numbers.

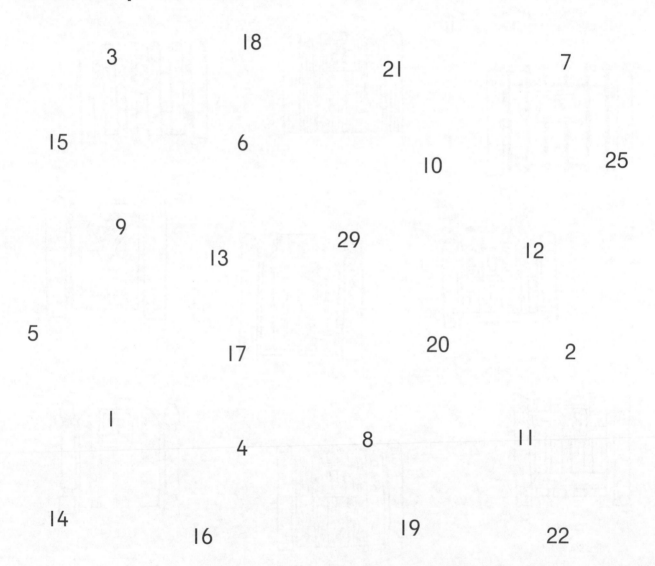

3   18   21   7

15   6   10   25

9   29   12

13

5   17   20   2

1

4   8   11

14   19   22

16

Describe in a sentence what prime numbers are.

_____

_____

Subtraction/addition, halving/doubling

Barry checks this addition **42 + 17 = 59**
with this subtraction **59 – 17 = 42**

Write an operation you could do to check these.

23 + 18 = 41   7 × 5 = 35   40 – 27 = 13

_____   _____   _____

17 – 8 = 9   18 + 23 = 41   18 × 2 = 36

_____   _____   _____

20 × 2 = 40   54 – 25 = 29   5 × 9 = 45

_____   _____   _____

26 + 14 + 18 = 58   14 + 15 + 16 = 45

_____   _____

17 + 19 = 36   19 × 2 = 38   40 × 2 = 80

_____   _____   _____

Sums and differences of odds and evens

Something odd here!

3 + 5 = ☐   5 + 9 = ☐   7 + 1 = ☐

21 + 17 = ☐   15 + 15 = ☐   23 + 17 = ☐

Now write a sentence about what happens when two odd numbers are added together.

_____

13 − 7 = ☐   15 − 3 = ☐   21 − 15 = ☐

45 − 15 = ☐   19 − 5 = ☐   17 − 3 = ☐

Now write a sentence about what happens when two odd numbers are subtracted.

_____

What will happen when two even numbers are subtracted?

_____

Appropriate operations/explain methods

$$+ \qquad - \qquad \times \qquad \div$$

Write a sign in the box to make each number fact correct.

7 ☐ 4 = 11   12 ☐ 5 = 7   2 ☐ 3 = 6

14 ☐ 7 = 7   20 ☐ 10 = 30   6 ☐ 5 = 30

20 ☐ 4 = 5   24 ☐ 16 = 8   50 ☐ 10 = 5

Make up a number story for each sum.

£1.20 + £1.60 = £2.80

_____

_____

28p + 54p + 12p = 94p

_____

_____

Solve 'real life' number problems

Find the numbers which obey these rules.

Two numbers add up to 10 but have a product of 24

Two numbers add up to 16 but have a product of 15

Use each number and sign once to make 30

| × + = 5 10 4 ( ) |

Use each number and sign once to make 250

| × + = 10 20 5 ( ) |

Patrick has some money. He spends 85p and has 25p left.
How much did he have to start with?

Hassan gave 25p to his brother and 25p to his sister. He
still has £1.75. How much did he have to start with?

Strategies for problem solving

Each item is half price in a sale. How much were they in the first place?

476 people go on the Millennium Wheel. Each pays £8.60. How much do they pay altogether?

Using each coin just once, how many different amounts can you make from these coins? Write down the amounts.

Solve problems with frequency tables

**Some children voted for their favourite Pikalot characters.
This frequency table shows the results.**

Favourite Pikalot	Number of votes
Smellybat	5
Goggrub	2
Bantilik	4
Snodge	0
Crumpy Dumpy	5
Rocodoco	8
Metalos	6

Which Pikalot did nobody vote for? _____

How many votes does Smellybat have? _____

Two Pikalots have the same vote. Which ones? _____

How many votes are there in total? _____

Does Metalos have more votes that Goggrub? _____

Who has the most votes? _____

Which Pikalots have fewer that 5 votes? _____

Collect, organise, present, interpret data

Animal farm

These are the animals kept on a small farm.

Show this information as a bar chart.

Write two questions you could answer with this information.

1. _____

_____

2. _____

_____

Extracting and interpreting data in tables

Year 6 Maths Test Results

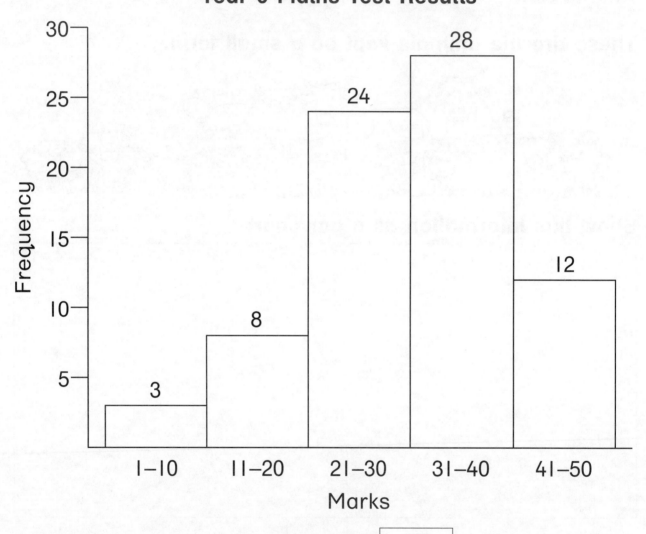

How many children took the test?

How many scored between 41 and 50 marks?

What was the most common score in the test?

Use of computer programs

These are the classroom temperatures during the day.

0800 10 °C	0900 15 °C	1000 18 °C	1100 21 °C
1200 25 °C	1300 28 °C	1400 31 °C	1500 30 °C
1600 27 °C	1700 24 °C	1800 16 °C	1900 12 °C

Draw a line graph to show this information.

Write two questions you could answer with this data.

1. _____

_____

2. _____

_____

Mean, median and mode

Mushrooms!

Some children are given soil and mushrooms. They keep count of how many mushrooms grow during one week. These are the results.

0 – one child

1 – no children

2 – one child

3 – five children

4 – eight children

5 – four children

6 – two children

7 – one child

What was the frequency of 5 mushrooms?

What was the range of the number of mushrooms?

Another class do the same thing but just keep count of the number of mushrooms grown. These are the results.

0 0 1 2 2 2 2 2 3 3 3 3 3 4 4 4 4 4 4 5 5 5 5 6 6 7 8 8 8 8 9

What was the frequency of 4 mushrooms?

What was the most common number (mode)?

What was the range of the number of mushrooms?

Discuss the likelihood of particular events

Write words like 'probable', 'likely', 'impossible', 'certain' and 'unlikely' to describe these events.

Superman will fly into the room to help me with my maths.

Time will run backwards.

Dad will win the lottery on Saturday.

My finger nails will grow.

A red car will go down the road.

A swordfish will win the London Marathon.

All the teachers are ill and we will be sent home.

The Martians will land in my garden!

Language of probability

With a partner, throw a 10p coin 50 times. Record how many times it lands heads and how many times tails.

Show the result on a bar graph.

What are equally likely outcomes when a coin is tossed?

Imagine a normal 1–6 dice is thrown. Answer these questions.

What is the probability of throwing a 6?

What is the probability of throwing an odd number?

What is the probability of throwing a 7?

Know the relationships between units

Help Jared join the measurements that are the same size as each other.

3500 g

1.5 m

50 cm

1000 g

1 km

1 l

4½ m

1 kg

2.5 kg   0.5 km

half a metre

1 kilogram

4.5 m

3.5 kg

0.5 m

½ kilometre

2500 g

3½ kg   450 cm

1 litre

500 m

one point five metres

½ m

1½ m   2½ kilograms

1000 m

1000 ml   four and a half metres

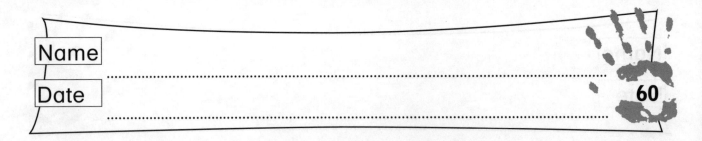

Equipment, resources and measures

Faith has to measure each thing. Join the things which have to be measured to the best instrument for the job.

Blueprints Maths Key Stage 2: Pupil Resource Book © Sean McArdle, Nelson Thornes Ltd, 2002

Drawing accurately and using equipment

Draw the lines using a ruler and pencil to the length shown.

3 cm

7 cm

2.5 cm

4.6 cm

43 mm

What is the perimeter of each shape? Write the answer in the box next to the shape.

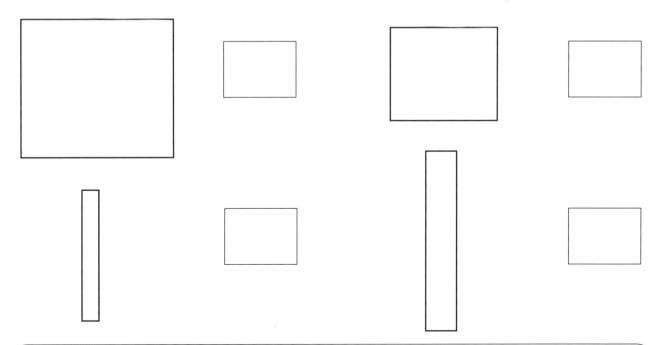

Imperial units

My weight

metric units _____

imperial units _____

My height

metric units _____

imperial units _____

My birth weight

metric units _____

imperial units _____

My favourite drink – capacity

metric units _____

imperial units _____

Blueprints Maths Key Stage 2: Pupil Resource Book © Sean McArdle, Nelson Thornes Ltd, 2002

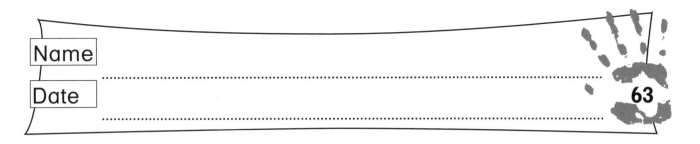

Decimal notation and £/p notation

Which is which? How many pennies does each child have?

Steve   Dalia   Stefan   Ingrid

£1.50   £3.70   £2.05   £5.48

How many centimetres?

Camilla Camel   Larry Lizard   Freda Frog   Wally Worm

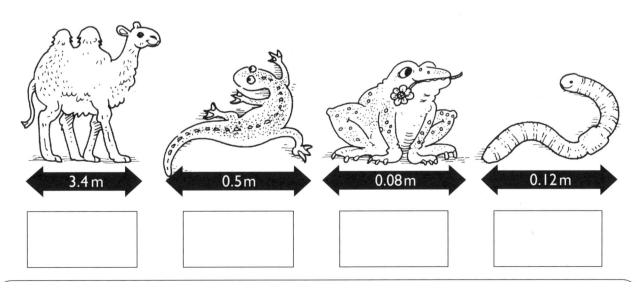

3.4m   0.5m   0.08m   0.12m

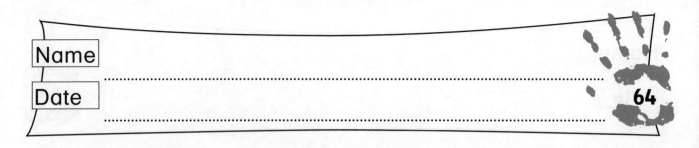

Read scales accurately

What length is shown?

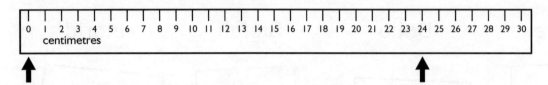

What measure is shown on this scale?

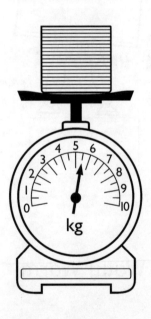

Show 725 g on this scale.

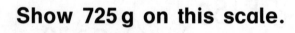
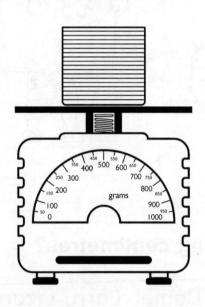

How much is in the jug?

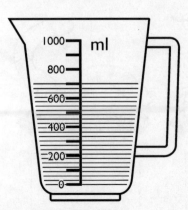

Show 950 ml on this jug.

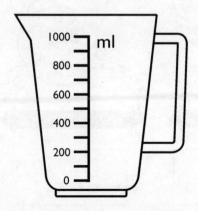

Read time to nearest 5 minutes/minute

Match the times on the watches on the left with the times on the digital displays.

Blueprints Maths Key Stage 2: Pupil Resource Book © Sean McArdle, Nelson Thornes Ltd, 2002

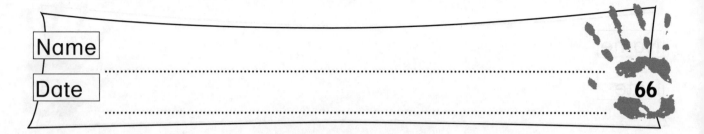

Name

Date

66

Use 24-hour clock notation

Complete the gaps in this table.

Event	Time		
Wake up in the morning	Half past seven	07:30	7:30 a.m.
Take the dog for a walk	Four o'clock in the afternoon		
Watch the evening news	Seven o'clock		
Go out for lunch	Quarter past twelve		
Put the cat out for the night	Ten past eleven		
Make breakfast	Quarter to eight		
Have haircut	Twenty past four in the afternoon		
Catch bus to work	Twenty-five to nine		8:35 a.m.
Play badminton in the evening	Half past seven		
Set the morning clock alarm	Six forty-five		
Have afternoon tea	Ten past five		
Take the children to school	Ten to nine		
Star watching	Eleven forty		
Midday meeting	Noon		

Measures

Teacher's Resource Book page 72

Blueprints Maths Key Stage 2: Pupil Resource Book © Sean McArdle, Nelson Thornes Ltd, 2002

Read simple timetables

Look at this timetable and then answer the questions.

	9.00–10.30	10.30–12.00	12.00 –1.00	1.00–2.30	2.30–3.30
Monday	Numeracy	Literacy	L	Science	Science
Tuesday	Numeracy	Literacy	U	History	History
Wednesday	Numeracy	Literacy	N	Music	Games
Thursday	Numeracy	Writing	C	Literacy	RE
Friday	Swimming	Numeracy	H	Literacy	PE

How many days do the children do Numeracy?

On which day is games?

Which lessons are between 1.00 and 2.30?

Which subject is in the morning and in the afternoon?

Which lesson follows swimming?

Blueprints Maths Key Stage 2: Pupil Resource Book © Sean McArdle, Nelson Thornes Ltd, 2002

Classify and describe 2-D and 3-D shapes

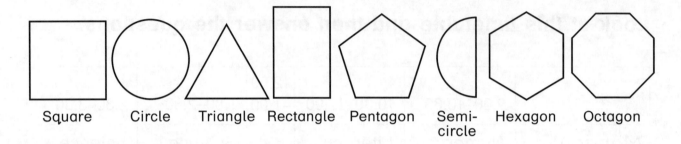

Square   Circle   Triangle   Rectangle   Pentagon   Semi-circle   Hexagon   Octagon

What am I?

I am half a circle.

I have three sides but not a right angle.

My five sides are the same length.

I have the same number of sides as an octopus has legs.

Give me a clue! Two shapes have not been named. Write clues to the two shapes.

_____

Name me

I am a solid shape with six faces made from squares.

I am the same shape as a ball but what is my mathematical name?

I have two identical triangular faces at opposite ends and my other faces are rectangles.

Classify and make polygons

Proper names please!

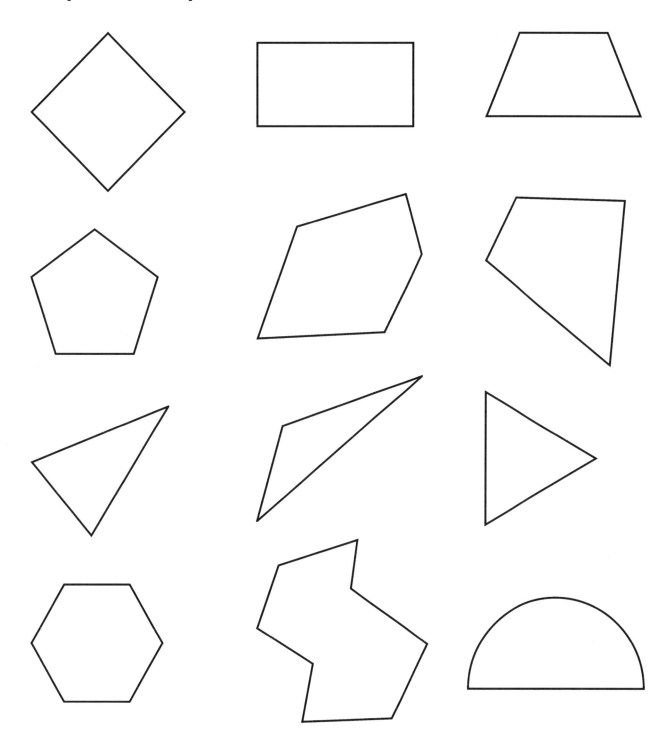

Line symmetry

Some of these shapes have line symmetry, some do not.
Which is which? Circle the shapes with line symmetry.

The missing half! Complete each shape.

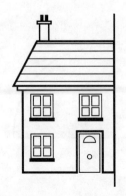
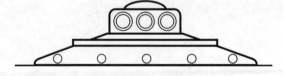

Blueprints Maths Key Stage 2: Pupil Resource Book © Sean McArdle, Nelson Thornes Ltd, 2002

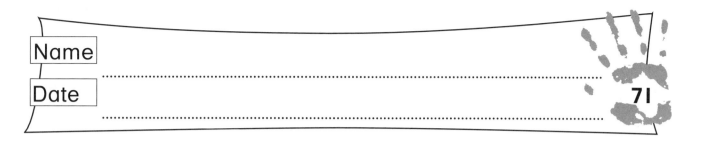

Reflective symmetry

Draw the lines of symmetry on each shape.

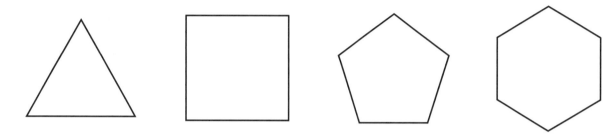

Write a rule about the number of lines of symmetry of regular polygons.

Sketch the reflection of each shape in the mirror.

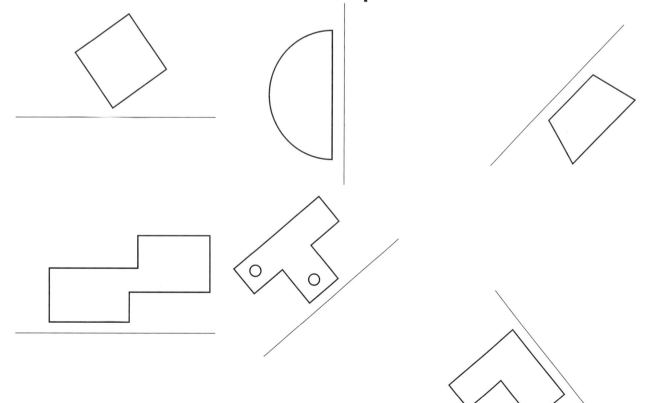

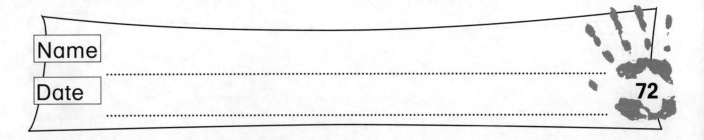

Shape translation

Move me! Translate each shape according to the instructions.

Translate the triangle 3 units down.

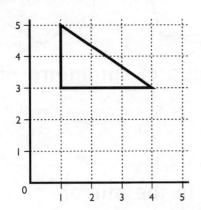

Translate the square 2 units to the left.

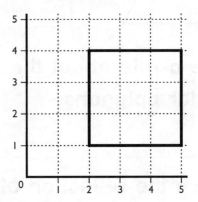

Translate the triangle 2 units up.

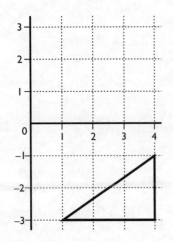

Translate the triangle 2 units up and 3 to the right.

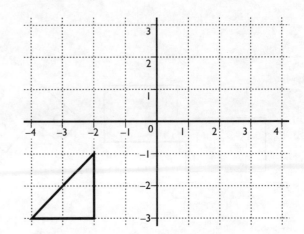

Blueprints Maths Key Stage 2: Pupil Resource Book © Sean McArdle, Nelson Thornes Ltd, 2002

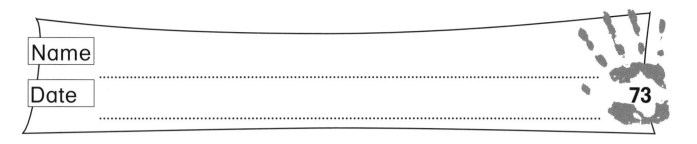

Shape rotation of 90°/180°

Move us too! Rotate each shape according to the instructions.

Sketch the position of the triangle after a clockwise rotation of 90° about A.

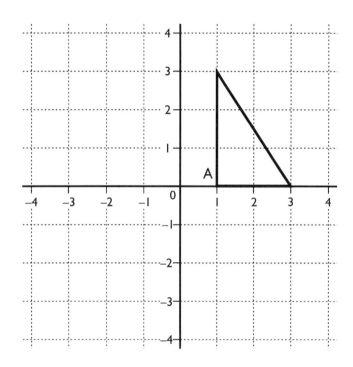

Sketch the position of the triangle after an anticlockwise rotation of 180° about A.

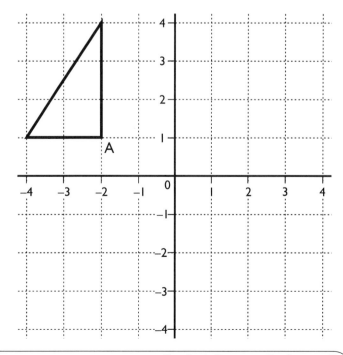

Blueprints Maths Key Stage 2: Pupil Resource Book © Sean McArdle, Nelson Thornes Ltd, 2002

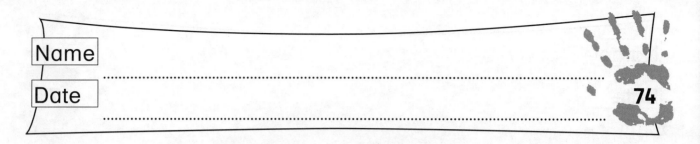

Recognise perpendicular and parallel lines

Look at the shapes and then answer the questions.

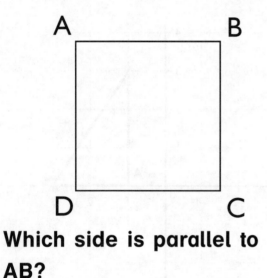

Which side is parallel to AB?

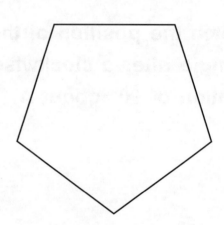

Are any sides perpendicular?

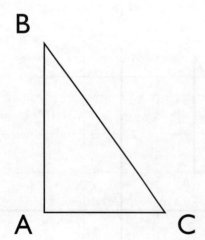

Which sides are perpendicular?

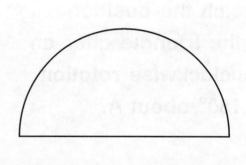

Are any sides parallel?

Blueprints Maths Key Stage 2: Pupil Resource Book © Sean McArdle, Nelson Thornes Ltd, 2002

Position using a grid

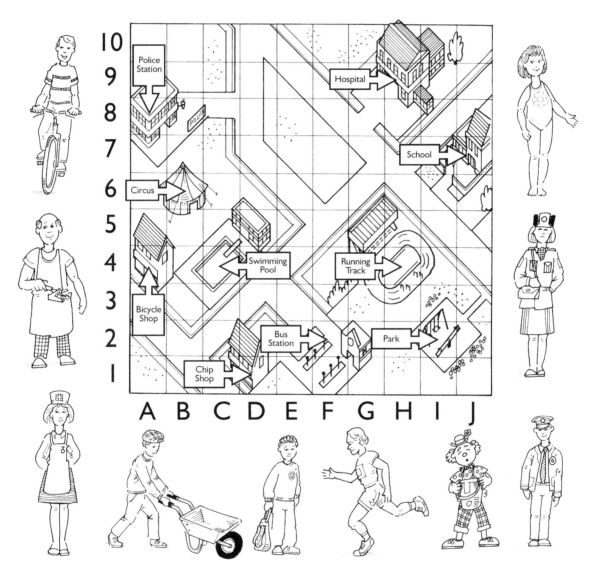

Write the position and building where each person has to go.

_____

_____

_____

_____

Blueprints Maths Key Stage 2: Pupil Resource Book © Sean McArdle, Nelson Thornes Ltd, 2002

Coordinates in all four quadrants

Give all the coordinates of the points between A and B.

Give the coordinates of the points between C and D.

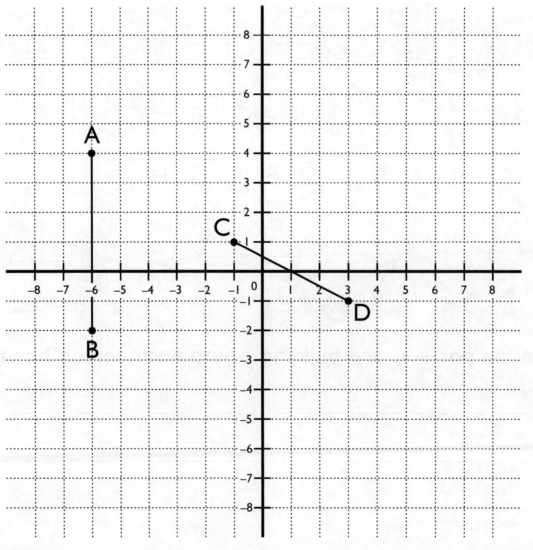

Angle as a measure of turn

Timed angles!

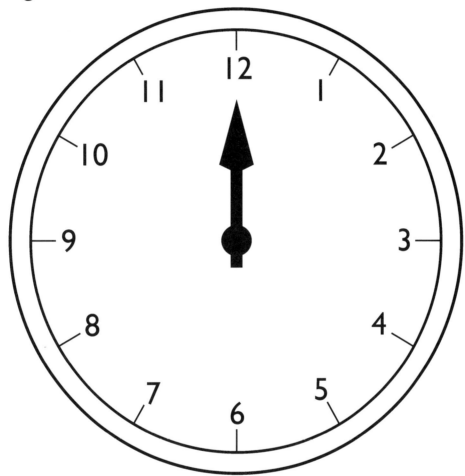

The hand makes one complete turn. How many degrees has it passed through?

The hand moves from 12 to 3. What is the name of the angle it has made?

The hand is pointing at 9 and then moves to 12. How many degrees has it moved through?

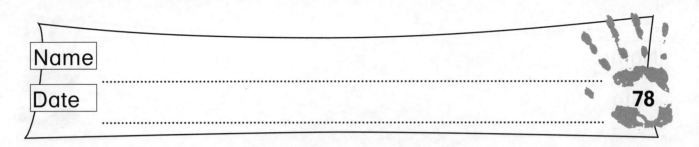

Use a protractor to nearest 5°

Big mouth! Use a protractor to measure the angle of the crocodile's mouth.

Fred

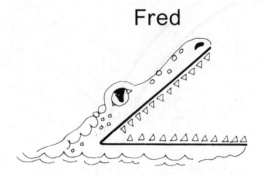

Annie

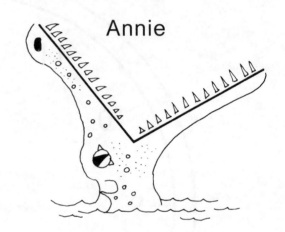

Emma

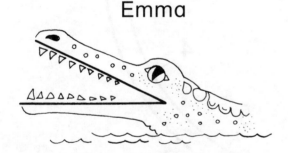

Dougal

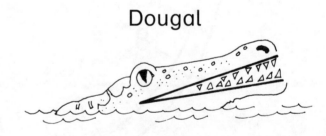

Cassie

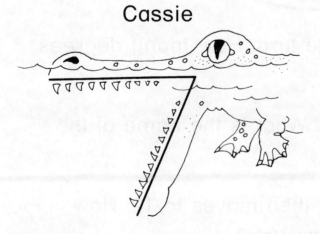

Sanjeet

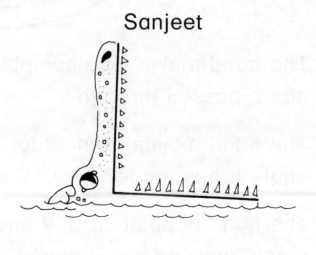

Who has the biggest mouth? _____

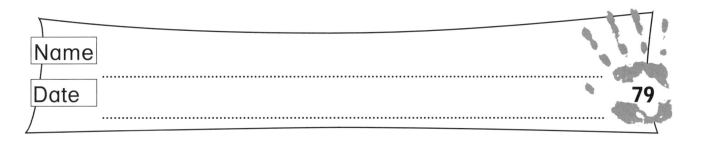

Use protractor to nearest degree

Measure the angle of each nose.

Zappo   Freda

Who has the widest nose? _____

Draw your own clowns with noses of these sizes. Name the clowns.

42°   153°

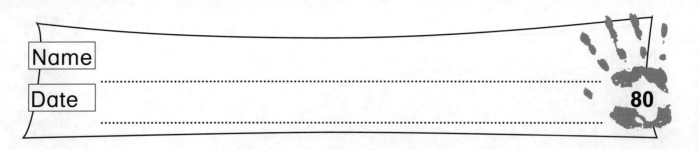

Angles

So many angles! Write either *acute*, *obtuse* **or** *right* **next to the monster's mouth.**

Draw three monster faces with mouths at these angles.

Acute angle	Obtuse angle	Right angle

Write in the size of the missing angle x.

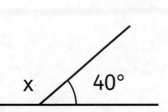

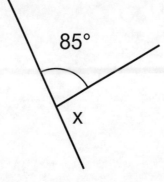

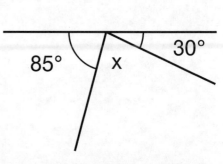

Nets of solid shapes

Complete the nets.

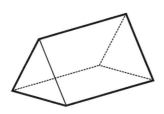

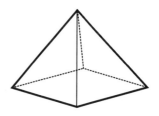

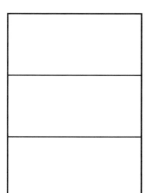

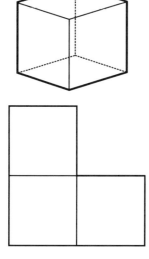

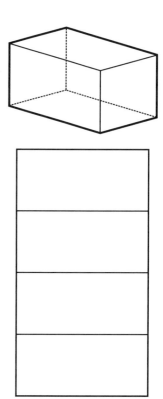

Perimeter

Measure the perimeter.

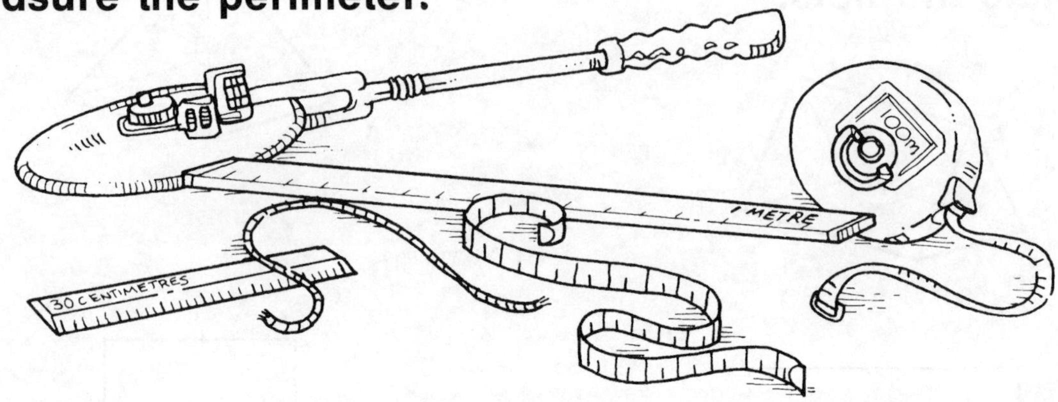

Choose the most suitable equipment for each job and then complete the table below.

The perimeter of ...	Measuring instrument	Estimate	Measured perimeter (include units)
My desk top			
My hand with fingers outstretched			
The school path			
My reading book			
The school hall			
The top of a paint pot			
The playground			
The top of a sandwich box			
My chair			
The computer keyboard			

Blueprints Maths Key Stage 2: Pupil Resource Book © Sean McArdle, Nelson Thornes Ltd, 2002

Area

Find my area!

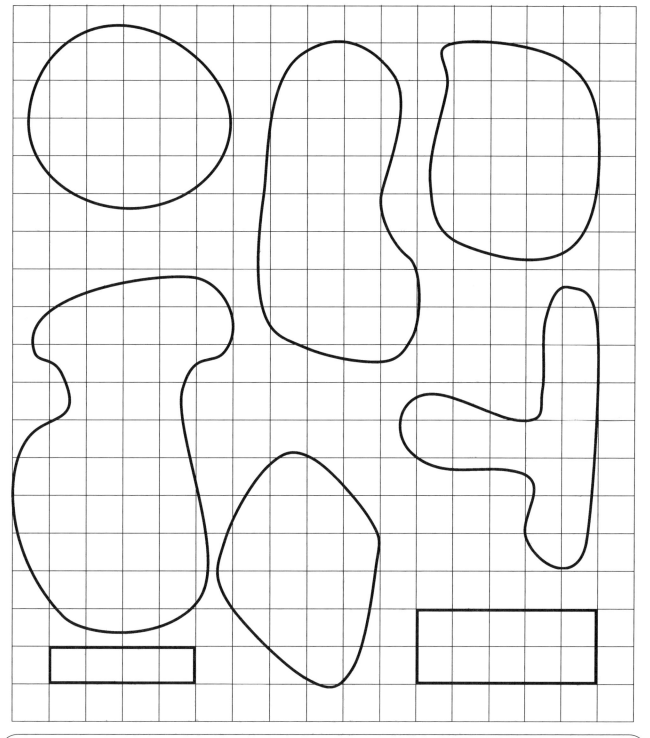

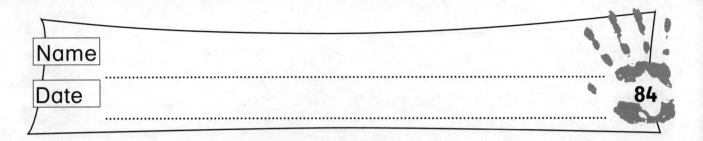

Area of compound shapes

Here are four car parks. Work out their areas and rank them in order of size.

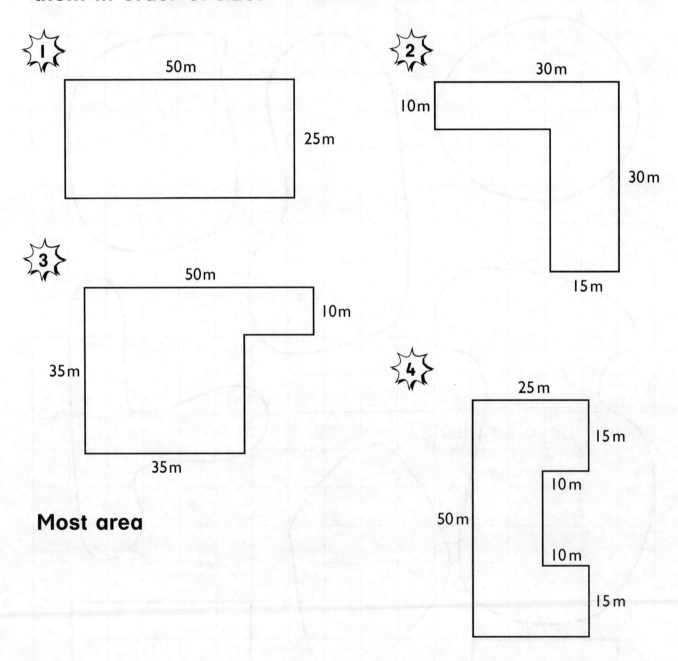

1   50m   25m

2   30m   10m   30m   15m

3   50m   10m   35m   35m

Most area

4   25m   15m   10m   50m   10m   15m

Least area

Visualise 3-D shapes from 2-D drawings

Troy and Helen need some open-top boxes. Which of these nets could they use to make the boxes?

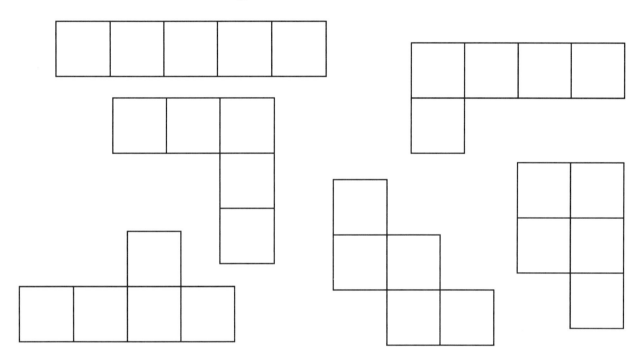

Doris needs to make a cube for a dice game. Only one of these nets could be used. Which one?

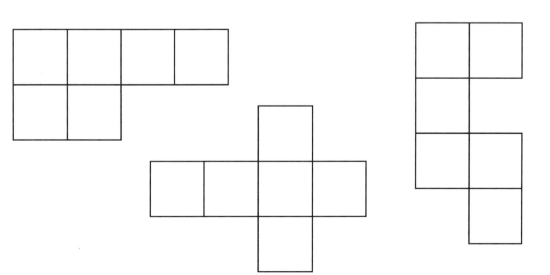

Vocabulary and properties of 2-D shapes

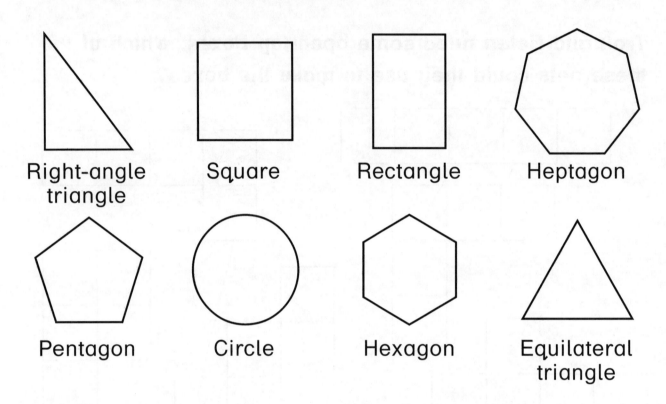

Right-angle triangle

Square

Rectangle

Heptagon

Pentagon

Circle

Hexagon

Equilateral triangle

Name the shapes which have at least one right angle.

Which shape has no line symmetry?

Which shape has the most line symmetry?

Which shapes are not regular?

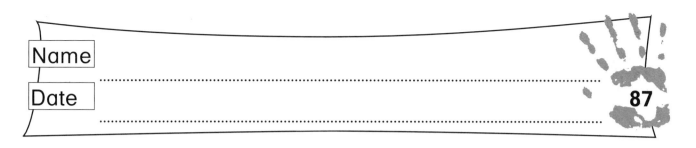

Sums of angles in a triangle

Accurately measure the angles in each shape to find the total.

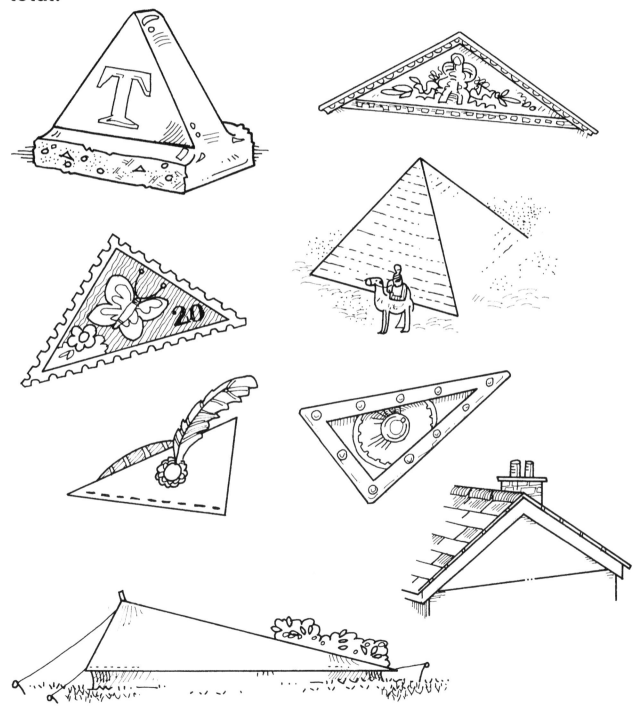

Blueprints Maths Key Stage 2: Pupil Resource Book © Sean McArdle, Nelson Thornes Ltd, 2002

0.5 cm squared graph paper

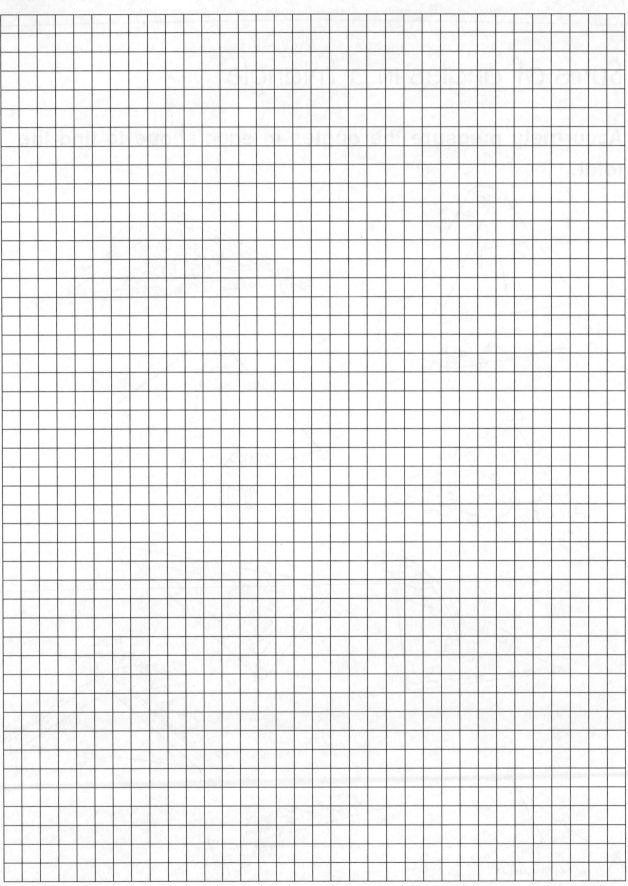

1 cm squared graph paper

2 cm squared graph paper

1–100 number square

1	2	3	4	5	6	7	8	9	10
11	12	13	14	15	16	17	18	19	20
21	22	23	24	25	26	27	28	29	30
31	32	33	34	35	36	37	38	39	40
41	42	43	44	45	46	47	48	49	50
51	52	53	54	55	56	57	58	59	60
61	62	63	64	65	66	67	68	69	70
71	72	73	74	75	76	77	78	79	80
81	82	83	84	85	86	87	88	89	90
91	92	93	94	95	96	97	98	99	100

1–31 calendar

Sunday	Monday	Tuesday	Wednesday	Thursday	Friday	Saturday
		1	2	3	4	5
6	7	8	9	10	11	12
13	14	15	16	17	18	19
20	21	22	23	24	25	26
27	28	29	30	31		

Carroll diagram blank

Coins and notes

1–100 number (words) square

one	two	three	four	five	six	seven	eight	nine	ten
eleven	twelve	thirteen	fourteen	fifteen	sixteen	seventeen	eighteen	nineteen	twenty
twenty-one	twenty-two	twenty-three	twenty-four	twenty-five	twenty-six	twenty-seven	twenty-eight	twenty-nine	thirty
thirty-one	thirty-two	thirty-three	thirty-four	thirty-five	thirty-six	thirty-seven	thirty-eight	thirty-nine	forty
forty-one	forty-two	forty-three	forty-four	forty-five	forty-six	forty-seven	forty-eight	forty-nine	fifty
fifty-one	fifty-two	fifty-three	fifty-four	fifty-five	fifty-six	fifty-seven	fifty-eight	fifty-nine	sixty
sixty-one	sixty-two	sixty-three	sixty-four	sixty-five	sixty-six	sixty-seven	sixty-eight	sixty-nine	seventy
seventy-one	seventy-two	seventy-three	seventy-four	seventy-five	seventy-six	seventy-seven	seventy-eight	seventy-nine	eighty
eighty-one	eighty-two	eighty-three	eighty-four	eighty-five	eighty-six	eighty-seven	eighty-eight	eighty-nine	ninety
ninety-one	ninety-two	ninety-three	ninety-four	ninety-five	ninety-six	ninety-seven	ninety-eight	ninety-nine	one hundred

1–31 ordinals

1 1st First	2 2nd Second	3 3rd Third
4 4th Fourth	5 5th Fifth	6 6th Sixth
7 7th Seventh	8 8th Eighth	9 9th Ninth
10 10th Tenth	11 11th Eleventh	12 12th Twelfth
13 13th Thirteenth	14 14th Fourteenth	15 15th Fifteenth
16 16th Sixteenth	17 17th Seventeenth	18 18th Eighteenth
19 19th Nineteenth	20 20th Twentieth	21 21st Twenty-first
22 22nd Twenty-second	23 23rd Twenty-third	24 24th Twenty-fourth
25 25th Twenty-fifth	26 26th Twenty-sixth	27 27th Twenty-seventh
28 28th Twenty-eighth	29 29th Twenty-ninth	30 30th Thirtieth
31 31st Thirty-first		

Metric/imperial conversion tables

Weight (mass)

Ounce (oz)	Gram (g)	Conversion to nearest 25 g
1	28	25
2	57	50
3	85	75
4 ($\frac{1}{4}$ lb)	113	125
5	142	150
6	170	175
7	198	200
8 ($\frac{1}{2}$ lb)	227	225
9	255	250
10	284	275
11	311	300
12 ($\frac{3}{4}$ lb)	340	350
13	368	375
14	396	400
15	425	425
16 (1 lb)	453	450
1 kilogram = 2.2 pounds		

Capacity (approximations)

1 litre = 0.22 gallons	
1 gallon = 4.5 litres	
1 litre = 1.76 pints	
1 pint = 0.56 litres	

Length (approximations)

1 centimetre = 0.4 inches	1 metre = 40 inches
1 metre = 1.1 yards	1 mile = 1.61 kilometres
1 millimetre = 0.4 inches	1 kilometre = 0.62 miles
1 inch = 2.54 centimetres	1 foot = 0.3 metres
1 yard = 0.9 metres	

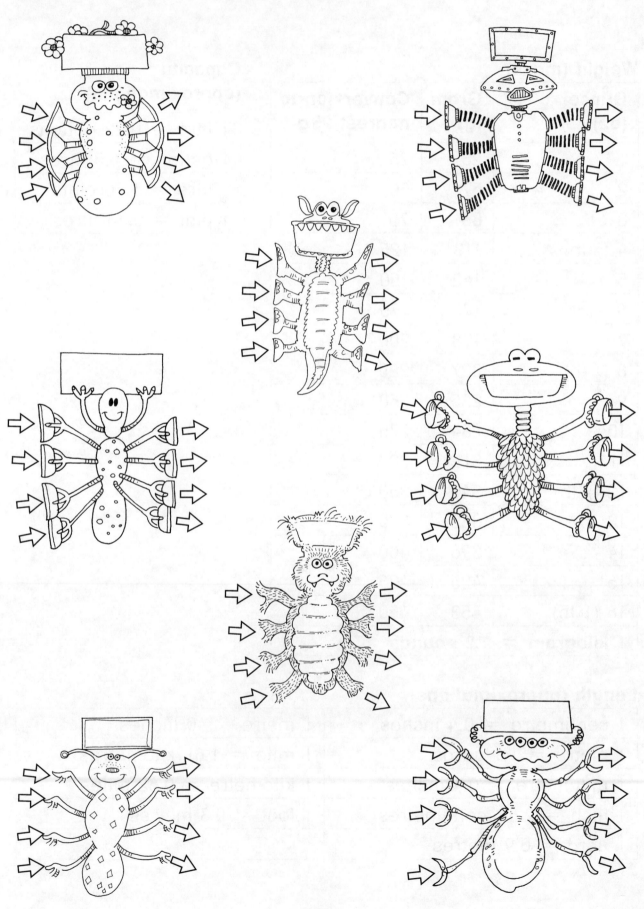

Fraction family

$\frac{1}{4}$	1 ÷ 4	0.25	25%
$\frac{1}{2}$	1 ÷ 2	0.5	50%
$\frac{3}{4}$	3 ÷ 4	0.75	75%
$\frac{1}{5}$	1 ÷ 5	0.2	20%
$\frac{2}{5}$	2 ÷ 5	0.4	40%
$\frac{3}{5}$	3 ÷ 5	0.6	60%
$\frac{4}{5}$	4 ÷ 5	0.8	80%
$\frac{1}{10}$	1 ÷ 10	0.1	10%
$\frac{2}{10}$	2 ÷ 10	0.2	20%
$\frac{3}{10}$	3 ÷ 10	0.3	30%
$\frac{4}{10}$	4 ÷ 10	0.4	40%
$\frac{5}{10}$	5 ÷ 10	0.5	50%
$\frac{6}{10}$	6 ÷ 10	0.6	60%
$\frac{7}{10}$	7 ÷ 10	0.7	70%
$\frac{8}{10}$	8 ÷ 10	0.8	80%
$\frac{9}{10}$	9 ÷ 10	0.9	90%

Measurement family

1 metre	1.0 m	100 cm	1000 mm
¾ metre	0.75 m	75 cm	750 mm
½ metre	0.5 m	50 cm	500 mm
¼ metre	0.25 m	25 cm	250 mm
1 litre	1 l	100 cl	1000 ml
¾ litre	0.75 l	75 cl	750 ml
½ litre	0.5 l	50 cl	500 ml
¼ litre	0.25 l	25 cl	250 ml
1 kilogram	1.0 kg	1000 g	1000 000 mg
¾ kilogram	0.75 kg	750 g	750 000 mg
½ kilogram	0.5 kg	500 g	500 000 mg
¼ kilogram	0.25 kg	250 g	250 000 mg

Record sheet (class teacher)

Child's name	Counting on or back in tens or hundreds	Counting in equal steps and in decimals	Read/write whole numbers to 1000/10 000	Know what each digit represents	Order whole numbers to 1000	Use symbols correctly including < and >	Order all symbols and to one million	Order positive and negative integers	Rounding to nearest ten and hundred	Recognise negative numbers in context	Positive and negative integers	Unit fractions	Simple fractions/equivalence	Simple fractions/find fractional parts	Begin to use ideas of simple proportion

Record sheet (class teacher)

Child's name	Mixed numbers and improper fractions	Reduce fractions by cancelling	Relate fractions to division	Decimal notation for tenths and hundredths	Order numbers with three decimal places	Equivalence between decimals and fractions	Round two decimal places to nearest integer	Percentage as number of parts in 100	Percentages of small whole numbers	Positive and negative facts to 20	Use informal pencil and paper methods	Begin to use column addition	Begin to use column subtraction	Column addition and subtraction	Short and long multiplication, short division

Record sheet (class teacher)

Child's name	Multiplication with decimals	Short division of numbers involving decimals	Addition and subtraction of decimals	Approximation methods	Calculator skills	Begin to use brackets	Division – inverse of multiplication	Begin to find remainders	Remainders	2×, 5×, 10× tables/3×, 4× tables	Begin to know 6×, 7×, 8×, 9× tables	All multiplication tables to 10× table	Numbers to 20, multiples of 5, 50, halves	All square numbers to 10 × 10/12 × 12	Factors to 100/prime factors

Record sheet (class teacher)

Child's name	Recognise prime numbers	Subtraction/addition, halving/doubling	Sums and differences of odds and evens	Appropriate operations/explain methods	Solve 'real life' number problems	Strategies for problem solving	Solve problems with frequency tables	Collect, organise, present, interpret data	Extracting and interpreting data in tables	Use of computer progams	Mean, median and mode	Discuss the likelihood of particular events	Language of probability	Know the relationships between units	Equipment, resources and measures

Record sheet (class teacher)

Child's name	Drawing accurately and using equipment	Imperial units	Decimal notation and £/p notation	Read scales accurately	Read time to nearest 5 minutes/minute	Use 24-hour clock notation	Read simple timetables	Classify and describe 2-D and 3-D shapes	Classify and make polygons	Line symmetry	Reflective symmetry	Shape translation	Shape rotation of 90°/180°	Recognise perpendicular and parallel lines	Position using a grid

Record sheet (class teacher)

Child's name	Coordinates in all four quadrants	Angle as a measure of turn	Use a protractor to nearest 5°	Use protractor to nearest degree	Angles	Nets of solid shapes	Perimeter	Area	Area of compound shapes	Visualise 3-D shapes from 2-D drawings	Vocabulary and properties of 2-D shapes	Sums of angles in a triangle			

Record sheet (supply teacher)

	School									
Counting on or back in tens or hundreds										
Counting in equal steps and in decimals										
Read/write whole numbers to 1000/10 000										
Know what each digit represents										
Order whole numbers to 1000										
Use symbols correctly including < and >										
Order all symbols and to one million										
Order positive and negative integers										
Rounding to nearest ten and hundred										
Recognise negative numbers in context										
Positive and negative integers										
Unit fractions										
Simple fractions/equivalence										
Simple fractions/find fractional parts										
Begin to use ideas of simple proportion										
Mixed numbers and improper fractions										
Reduce fractions by cancelling										
Relate fractions to division										
Decimal notation for tenths and hundredths										
Order numbers with three decimal places										
Equivalence between decimals and fractions										
Round two decimal places to nearest integer										

Record sheet (supply teacher)

	School								
Percentage as number of parts in 100									
Percentages of small whole numbers									
Positive and negative facts to 20									
Use informal pencil and paper methods									
Begin to use column addition									
Begin to use column subtraction									
Column addition and subtraction									
Short and long multiplication, short division									
Multiplication with decimals									
Short division of numbers involving decimals									
Addition and subtraction of decimals									
Approximation methods									
Calculator skills									
Begin to use brackets									
Division – inverse of multiplication									
Begin to find remainders									
Remainders									
2×, 5×, 10× tables/3×, 4× tables									
Begin to know 6×, 7×, 8×, 9× tables									
All multiplication tables to 10× table									
Numbers to 20, multiples of 5, 50, halves									
All square numbers to 10 × 10/12 × 12									

Record sheet (supply teacher)

	School										
Factors to 100/prime factors											
Recognise prime numbers											
Subtraction/addition, halving/doubling											
Sums and differences of odds and evens											
Appropriate operations/explain methods											
Solve 'real life' number problems											
Strategies for problem solving											
Solve problems with frequency tables											
Collect, organise, present, interpret data											
Extracting and interpreting data in tables											
Use of computer progams											
Mean, median and mode											
Discuss the likelihood of particular events											
Language of probability											
Know the relationships between units											
Equipment, resources and measures											
Drawing accurately and using equipment											
Imperial units											
Decimal notation and £/p notation											
Read scales accurately											
Read time to nearest 5 minutes/minute											
Use 24-hour clock notation											

Record sheet (supply teacher)

	School									
Read simple timetables										
Classify and describe 2-D and 3-D shapes										
Classify and make polygons										
Line symmetry										
Reflective symmetry										
Shape translation										
Shape rotation of 90°/180°										
Recognise perpendicular and parallel lines										
Position using a grid										
Coordinates in all four quadrants										
Angle as a measure of turn										
Use a protractor to nearest 5°										
Use protractor to nearest degree										
Angles										
Nets of solid shapes										
Perimeter										
Area										
Area of compound shapes										
Visualise 3-D shapes from 2-D drawings										
Vocabulary and properties of 2-D shapes										
Sums of angles in a triangle										

Answers

(unnumbered sums on the activity sheets should be read left to right)

Activity
sheet

3 *Which year?*
213   1066   1509

Lots of money
Eight thousand, one hundred and five pounds
Six thousand and seven pounds
Three thousand, four hundred and sixty pounds

4 *Complete this sequence*
234
700
600   5

5 345   636   869   590
230   421   967   426

65p   80p   £850
£730   130p   110p

122   124   126   128
66   68   70   72   74   76   78
2.5 kg   52 cm   103 cm

245   254   452   524   542
76   607   670   706   760

8 *Negative numbers*
−1   −4   −5   −6   −8   −10

Positve numbers
3   5   7   10   12

9 20   40   70   80   30
230   210   110   180   160
400   300   100   200
600   700   400   800

10 *Below 0 °C*
Scotland   Finland   Poland

Warmer than Scotland/colder than Spain
Holland   Germany

Colder than Poland
Scotland   Finland

11 6   3.4   13   19   240   80   3

12 Sanchez 5p   Maria 4p
Alfonse 10p   Danielle 6p

3 cars   6 bees
8 raindrops   4 shoes

13 $\frac{5}{6}$ $\frac{7}{10}$ $\frac{3}{7}$

$\frac{4}{8}$ or $\frac{2}{4}$ or $\frac{1}{2}$ $\frac{2}{6}$ or $\frac{1}{3}$ $\frac{3}{9}$ or $\frac{1}{3}$

14 $\frac{1}{10}$ $\frac{1}{4}$ $\frac{1}{2}$ $\frac{3}{4}$

$\frac{1}{5}$ $\frac{2}{5}$ $\frac{3}{5}$ $\frac{4}{5}$

$\frac{1}{10}$ $\frac{1}{4}$ $\frac{1}{3}$ $\frac{1}{2}$

$\frac{2}{10}$ $\frac{4}{10}$ $\frac{5}{10}$ $\frac{9}{10}$

3   5   10   4   8
5   3   7   6   10
4   1   6   9   5
6   1   10   3   8
4 kg   8 kg   1 kg   100 kg
12
20
20
15
21
45

15 10   25   15   35   60
4   7   20   3   16
6   20

16 $1\frac{1}{2}$ $2\frac{1}{2}$ $4\frac{1}{2}$

$2\frac{1}{3}$ 4   10

10    $4\frac{1}{4}$ 9

$\frac{7}{2}$ $\frac{15}{2}$ $\frac{19}{2}$

$\frac{53}{2}$ $\frac{13}{3}$ $\frac{28}{3}$

$\frac{38}{3}$ $\frac{62}{3}$ $\frac{63}{5}$

$4\frac{3}{5}$ or 4.6 $3\frac{7}{10}$ or $\frac{37}{10}$ $\frac{63}{10}$ or 6.3

17 $\frac{1}{4}$ $\frac{1}{10}$ $\frac{1}{2}$

$\frac{9}{10}$ $\frac{2}{3}$ $\frac{1}{50}$

$\frac{1}{6}$ $\frac{4}{5}$ $\frac{9}{10}$

$\frac{1}{6}$ $\frac{1}{4}$ $\frac{7}{8}$

$\frac{1}{5}$ $\frac{2}{15}$ $\frac{2}{5}$

$\frac{3}{25}$ $\frac{1}{3}$ $\frac{1}{6}$

$\frac{5}{18}$ $\frac{4}{5}$ $\frac{19}{36}$

18 15   11   25
36   11   15
7   20   18
18   80   13
20   45   15
20   23   15

19 0.3   0.07   0.2   0.05
0.1   0.9   0.4   0.2
0.5   0.7   0.9   0.6

165p   273p   550p   109p

£2.05   £3.41   £5.60   £0.56

0.65   2.84   3.12   5.07

Answers

20
2751 m	3750 ml	5000 g	60 ml
0.76 m	0.856 m	2.67 m	12.531 m
0.248 kg	2.048 kg	2.485 kg	24.851 kg
0.551 m	5.051 m	5.51 m	50.51 m
20.054	20.07	20.454	20.7
1.049	1.5	5.049	5.1
0.009	0.041	0.101	0.321

22
£2	£3	£1
£2	£4	£4

2 m	3 m	19 m
45 m	7 m	30 m

3 kg	7 kg	1 kg
7 kg	1 kg	13 kg

6 l	3 l	4 l
12 l	15 l	1 l

23
5p	10p	1p	50p	25p

3 cm	4.5 cm	2.5 cm

6p	30p	100p

24
0.25 and $\frac{1}{4}$ 0.4 and $\frac{4}{10}$ or $\frac{2}{5}$

0.68 and $\frac{68}{100}$ or $\frac{34}{50}$ or $\frac{17}{25}$ 0.1 and $\frac{1}{10}$

0.75 and $\frac{3}{4}$ 0.18 and $\frac{18}{100}$ or $\frac{9}{50}$

10% $\frac{1}{5}$ 0.2

£54   £240

25
1 + 15	2 + 14	3 + 13	4 + 12
5 + 11	6 + 10	7 + 9	8 + 8

1 + 16	2 + 15	3 + 14	4 + 13
5 + 12	6 + 11	7 + 10	8 + 9

6	8	15
15	9	5
14	5	12
3	17	0

26 74   93   18   27

27
49p	29p	62p	39p
197p	298p	191p	369p
380p	400p	845p	505p

28
22p	23p	50p	52p
9p	29p	4p	18p
26p	77p	61p	75p

29
7322	4768	3301
3785	9647	8426
7536	13 157	4183
4037	1677	1870

30
580	711	870
1296	4344	12 558
38 750	57 876	15 950
49	65	127

31
17.0	22.8	15.2
9.0	53.0	86.8
43.5	129.6	107.2
227.4	298.2	405.6

32
67.75	20.5	46.2
96	52.75	63.6
88.33	46	87
158.25	65.33	56

33
£11.85	£13.75	£9.17
£13.91	£13.72	£9.95
£11.30	£14.52	£8.80
£13.85	£4.33	£7.32

34
$32 \times 10 = 320$
$17 \times 10 = 170$
$27 \times 10 = 270$
$11 \times 10 = 110$
$36 \times 20 = 720$
$40 \times 20 = 800$ or $41 \times 20 = 820$
$20 \times 10 = 200$
$21 \times 10 = 210$

35
63, 64, 65
83 and 20 ml left
2 097 151p or £20 971.51
3.14
£2.05

36 *Corrected wrong calculations*
$2 \times (3 + 5) = 16$ $15 + (10 - 6) = 19$
$20 - (10 + 3) = 7$
$10 \times (5 - 4) = 10$ $(3 \times 4) + 2 = 14$
$(8 - 3) \times 2 = 10$ $(2 \times 6) - 3 = 9$
$14 - (3 \times 4) = 2$ $20 + (5 \times 3) = 35$
$16 - (5 + 6) = 5$ $20 - (4 \times 3) = 8$
$15 + (3 \times 2) = 21$ $60 - (6 + 6) = 48$

37
$4 \times 3 = 12$	$2 \times 5 = 10$	$2 \times 4 = 8$
$12 \div 3 = 4$	$10 \div 5 = 2$	$8 \div 4 = 2$
$12 \div 4 = 3$	$10 \div 2 = 5$	$8 \div 2 = 4$

$5 \times 3 = 15$	$12 \div 4 = 3$	$20 \div 4 = 5$
$15 \div 3 = 5$	$3 \times 4 = 12$	$5 \times 4 = 20$
$15 \div 5 = 3$	$4 \times 3 = 12$	$4 \times 5 = 20$

$16 \div 8 = 2$	$20 \div 10 = 2$	$10 \times 5 = 50$
$8 \times 2 = 16$	$2 \times 10 = 20$	$50 \div 10 = 5$
$2 \times 8 = 16$	$10 \times 2 = 20$	$50 \div 5 = 10$

38
1	1	2
none	none	1

39
2	6	16
2	1	
2p	5p	2p

40
10	40	20
40	14	18
14	12	14
12	80	80

Answers

80	12	45
12	45	24
45	9	21
100	10	16
10	35	90

41

24	21	49
21	40	81
40	18	64
18	49	36
36	63	72
63	56	42
56	45	72
45	18	56
18	24	54

42

12	54	18
45	28	24
56	48	28
30	63	30
54	12	54
16	56	70
32	54	64
54	81	63
28	49	40

44 4   9   16   25   36   49   64
81   100   121

45 6 = 1, 2, 3, 6   15 = 1, 3, 5, 15
9 = 1, 3, 9   20 = 1, 2, 4, 5, 10, 20
11 = 1, 11   50 = 1, 2, 5, 10, 25, 50
81 = 1, 3, 9, 27, 81   17 = 1, 17
92 = 1, 2, 4, 23, 46, 92

46 1   3   5   7   11
13   17   19   23   29
(1 is sometimes considered prime)

47 41 − 18 =   35 ÷ 5 =   40 − 13 =
41 − 23 =   35 ÷ 7 =   27 + 13 =

17 − 9 =   41 − 23 =   36 ÷ 2 =
8 + 9 =   41 − 18 =   36 ÷ 18 =

40 ÷ 2 =   25 + 29 =   45 ÷ 9 =
40 ÷ 20 =   54 − 29 =   45 ÷ 5 =

14 + 18 + 26 =   16 + 14 + 15 =
18 + 14 + 26 =   15 + 16 + 14 =

36 − 17 = 19   38 ÷ 2 = 19
36 − 19 = 17   38 ÷ 19 = 2

80 ÷ 2 = 40
80 ÷ 40 = 2

Wrong answers
46 − 27   45 × 2
26 + 45   45 × 2 = 80

48 8   14   8
38   30   40

When two odd numbers are added together, the resulting number is always even.

6   12   6
30   14   14

When two odd numbers are subtracted, the resulting answer is always even.

When two even numbers are subtracted, the resulting number is always even.

49 +   −   ×
−   +   ×
÷   −   ÷

50 4 and 6
1 and 15
(10 − 4) × 5
(5 + 20) × 10
£1.10
£2.25

51 £55.70   £37.98   £4093.60

15 *amounts*:
1p
2p
5p
10p
3p (1p + 2p)
6p (1p + 5p)
11p (1p + 10p)
7p (2p + 5p)
12p (2p + 10p)
15p (5p + 10p)
8p (1p + 2p + 5p)
13p (1p + 2p +10p)
16p (1p + 5p + 10p)
17p (2p + 5p +10p)
18p (1p + 2p + 5p + 10p)

52 Snodge
5
Smellybat and Crumpy Dumpy
30
yes
Rocodoco
Goggrub, Bantilik and Snodge

54 75
12
between 31 and 40

56 4
0 to 7 (7)
7
4
0–9 (9)

Answers

57 (Alternative words may be used.
Some statements are worth debating.)

Impossible
Impossible
Possible/unlikely
Certain
Probable/likely
Impossible
Unlikely
Impossible

58 Children should write words to the effect that landing heads or tails is equally likely and that with 50 throws, 25 of each could be expected.

1 in 6
3 in 6 or 1 in 2
nil

61 11 cm   15.6 cm   8 cm   11.4 cm

63 150p   370p   205p   548p
340 cm   50 cm   8 cm   12 cm

64 24 cm   5.5 kg   700 ml

66
16.00	4.00 p.m.
19.00	7.00 p.m.
12.15	12.15 p.m.
11.10	11.10 a.m.
07.45	7.45 a.m.
16.20	4.20 p.m.
08.35	8.35 a.m.
19.30	7.30 p.m.
06.45	6.45 a.m.
17.10	5.10 p.m.
08.50	8.50 a.m.
23.40	11.40 p.m.
12.00	12 noon

67 5 days
Wednesday
Science, History, Music, Literacy
Literacy
Numeracy

68 semicircle
equilateral triangle
pentagon
octagon

cube
sphere
triangular prism

69 square   rectangle
trapezium   regular pentagon
irregular pentagon quadrilateral
isoceles triangle   scalene triangle
equilateral triangle regular hexagon
irregular octagon   semicircle

70 symmetric   not symmetric
symmetric   not symmetric
not symmetric   not symmetric

71 the equilateral triangle has three possible lines
the square has four possible lines
the pentagon has five possible lines
the hexagon has six possible lines

The children might write something like 'Regular 2-D shapes have the same number of lines of symmetry as they do sides'.

74 DC   no
AB and AC   no

75 boy on bike to A4
swimmer to C4
policewoman to A8
bus driver to G2
clown to B6
runner to H4
schoolchild to J7
man pushing wheelbarrow to I1
nurse to H9
person selling chips to D1

76 (−6,3), (−6,2), (−6,1), (−6,0), and (−6,1)

$(0,\frac{1}{2})$, (1,0) and $(2,-\frac{1}{2})$

77 360°
right angle
90°

78 40°   100°   25°
10°   65°   90°
Annie

79 Freda

80 right   obtuse   obtuse   acute
140°   95°   65°

83 Approximate answers
19 cm²   28 cm²   22 cm²   40 cm²
16 cm²   4 cm²   18 cm²   10 cm²

84 (1) is 1250 m²
(2) is 600 m²
(3) is 1375 m²
(4) is 1050 m²

85 4th and 5th nets   2nd net

86 right-angle triangle, square, rectangle
right-angle triangle
circle (infinite)
right-angle triangle and rectangle